jambalaya for the soul

jambalaya for the Soul

Humorous Stories and Cajun Recipes from the Bayou

by Dr. Jesse Duplantis

Jesse Duplantis Ministries
New Orleans, Louisiana

05 04 03 02   10 9 8 7 6

Jambalaya for the Soul—
Humorous Stories and Cajun Recipes From the Bayou
ISBN 1-57794-304-X
Copyright © 2000 by Jesse Duplantis
PO Box 20149
New Orleans, Louisiana 70141

Published by Jesse Duplantis Ministries
PO Box 20149
New Orleans, Louisiana 70141

Contents

DEDICATION

Thank you to my wife, Cathy, for living through some of these stories with me, for always being behind what God's called me to do and for always saying, "I'm wicha, Jesse!" every step of the way. To my daughter, Jodi, for helping me over the years turn what I preach into what can be read! And to my son-in-law, Eddie, whose original idea to make a tape series of "the funny stuff" brought about this book today.

To everyone who contributed recipes for the book, I want to say a special thanks. The world needs our stuff; it's a bland world out there!

Thanks also to my sister-in-law, Christine, for gathering all the family recipes for this book and, of course, for including her famous banana pudding. To my brother, Wayne, and my sister, Debra, for contributing some of our side of the family's recipes—including some of Mama's. (She'd flip to see her stuff in here!) And last but not least, thanks go to one of the best cooks I know—my mother-in-law, Irene. Nobody, and I mean nobody, can cook an oyster gumbo like you! I'm grateful for every spoonful you've ever made me!

My special thanks to everyone who had a part in this book—especially the Harrison House family, who worked so hard to get it done. I appreciate you all.

INTRODUCTION

The Bible says, **A merry heart doeth good like a medicine: but a broken spirit drieth the bones** (Proverbs 17:22). I want to invite you to be blessed as you read the following stories. I believe they'll make you laugh, make you shout, make you rejoice, make you do all kinds of crazy things! You're probably going to see me in all different lights as I tell the stories of my life. But I hope you'll be blessed. Realize that being a Christian isn't dull—sometimes it's crazy! So get ready to sit down and laugh!

But before you read on, I want you to know something. Every time I've preached the gospel, I didn't say something funny just for it to be funny. There's always a point behind it. So get ready to laugh, but also get ready to get healed and blessed and stirred up for the Lord. Yes, sir, I believe that'll happen. Why? Because a merry heart does good like a medicine! And if you've got a broken spirit that's drying them old bones up, we'll put some joy juices in there and open you up to the strengthening joy of the Lord!

So you get ready to laugh—*and* be ministered to. Go get a box of popcorn and a Coke, and sit down and enjoy!

1

FEAR OF A HEADLESS CHICKEN

I had a wonderful grandfather. I would say he was probably one of the best grandfathers a boy could ever have.

When he was only five years old, his mother left him on a New Orleans street wharf. He turned around to look for her, and suddenly he had no mom. He was in trouble, so he walked down to this old Cajun fisherman and said, "Listen, ah, can I go to work on your boat?" He was five years old when he did that! He knew he was in trouble. But that man took him in and raised him.

My grandfather grew up to be a very strong, robust fisherman. He wore a size fifteen ring, and his fingers were as thick as carrots. His hands were wide and powerful, you know, from pulling shrimp nets.

He was a tough man, and I idolized him. I called him Paw-paw.

Paw-paw loved oranges. When I was growing up, we lived down in Venice, Louisiana, about ninety miles south of New Orleans. Venice had orange trees, and since Paw-paw loved oranges, he would say, "Jesse, go up that tree and get me some oranges." I'd go up those orange trees and just rip oranges from the branches, knocking him in the head with them. Afterward, he would just sit there and eat them, one after another. He just loved them.

Now, what we were doing was *stealing* those oranges. My grandpa wasn't saved, and neither was his grandson. You've got to understand—we didn't know we were sinning by doing that.

Once, when both my mother and father had some business to do, they let us stay with Paw-paw for a couple of days. When we got there, he said, "Boys, we gonna eat some chicken. Your grandma's gonna fry some chicken with some gravy."

And I went, "Whooooooo! Yeah, I like that, you know."

He said, "Come on with me, Jesse, I want to show you something."

Now, let me tell you something. We were very, very poor people, and in those days when you wanted a chicken—we called it a fryer—you didn't go to the grocery store to get it. You went in your backyard to the chicken coop. You know what I'm talking about? You ever gone out back to get a chicken? All the people around there raised their own chickens, killed them, plucked the feathers out and cleaned them. You did whatever you needed to do to eat those chickens.

So Paw-paw and I walked back to the chicken coop to get a chicken. Now, those chickens my grandpa had were the meanest chickens you ever saw. Every one of them was demon possessed. I hated those chickens. Every time I got around those chickens, they'd go, *Rhhhhh rhhhh,* and then they'd attack. They were mean as dogs. They'd just come at me, *Fwwww fwwwwww* and kick me with their feet. They were just plain mean chickens—I'd swear they were demon-possessed chickens. You know, they were raggedy looking demon chickens.

When I went into the chicken coop, I said, "I don't want 'em to bite me, Paw-paw."

"Stay behind me, boy," he said. He weighed 260 pounds and was a huge man. So I got behind him, like he said, and he told me, "Now, Jesse, go shoo that chicken into the corner."

"No!" I said. "He's gonna bite me. I don't wanta. I don't wanta shoo that chicken!"

"Come on, son," he said. "Boy, you're part of my life. You've got spitfire in your body. Now get over there and shoo that chicken!"

I crept out from behind my grandpa and quietly started saying, "Shoo, shoo. Shoo, shoo." And by some miracle I got one of those chickens backed into the corner.

"Catch him!" my grandpa said. "Catch him, boy!"

"No!" I said. "I ain't putting my hand on that chicken. That was not in the deal. You just told me to shoo him into the corner. I shooed him in the corner—now you catch him, Paw-paw."

When my grandpa went after that chicken, the chicken knew he was a goner. You could see the terror in that chicken's eyes. It was going, *God, forgive me. Today I'll meet You face to face, with a Cajun chewing on my leg as I go to heaven.*

Paw-paw grabbed that chicken and said, "Go get me the hatchet, Jesse." So, man, I ran to get that thing to give it to my grandpa. I was about to see something I had never seen in my life. Never! Paw yelled, "I'm going to show you something, son."

"What are you going to do?" I asked.

"Watch this," he said. He laid that chicken down on the ground and picked up that little hatchet. Paw-paw was looking at me, and then he got a little smile like he was thinking, *Heh, heh, heh. You're going to see something now, boy.*

When he raised the hatchet, I cried, "What're you going to do, Paw-paw?"

"Just watch, Jess," he said. And *boom!* Down came his arm with that hatchet. But the chicken went *thhhhck* and sucked his neck in.

He missed the chicken!

I looked at him and said, "Paw-paw, you missed him!"

"Isn't that something?" he said.

"I'd pull my head in too," I said. He looked at me, smiling, but I was still nervous. Those other chickens were nervous too. They were all screaming, *Brrrrrrrk, brrrrrk.* Murder was in the camp, and they knew it. But I didn't.

So he picked up the hatchet again, laid that bird down and said, "Watch, Jesse."

Now, I was a little fellow, about knee-high, but I was watching really closely. Paw-paw raised the hatchet over his head and brought it down again. *Thhhhck* went the chicken's neck, and *wham!* went the hatchet into the ground.

"Paw-paw, you missed him again."

"I'm going to get him this time," he said, and with his big foot, he stepped right on that chicken's head.

Rohhhhhhhhk!

That's the last thing that chicken ever said. I know what it meant: "Father, forgive me—I've sinned."

Grandpa came down with the hatchet, and this time he didn't miss. *Whack!* The head came off, and man, the blood spurted everywhere. I went, "Ahhhhhhhh!" and took a few steps back. Paw-paw looked over and threw the dead chicken at me.

I got up and ran so fast, crying, "Ohhhhh!" And everywhere I ran, that chicken ran after me. I mean, I ran to this spot, and here came that chicken. Blood was spurting out of his neck. Everywhere I ran, that dead chicken ran after me. How many people have seen that before?

I was going, "Ahhhhhhhhh, ahhhhhhhhh!" Finally I got up against the fence. My grandpa was laughing the whole time. "Jesse, that chicken's dead," he said.

"He don't know he's dead!" I yelled. "He don't know he's dead. Look at him!"

That dead chicken ran me all over the coop. He got right up to me in the corner and then just fell over, lifeless. I looked down, raised my foot behind me and punted that chicken. *Bam!* I was never so glad to see a dead chicken dead!

Now, that chicken was dead, but he was still running. A lot of Christians don't realize that it's the same way with the devil. Let me tell you, the devil's head has been bruised, and he's under your feet, bless God. You can destroy every plan the devil tries to form against you. He is just a little chicken, bluffing us with his wings.

Get your foot on the devil's neck! You'll never crush his head till you put your foot on him. The Bible says Satan's head is bruised. (Romans 16:20.) That means he's restricted, rejected and defeated. How can you get overwhelmed by circumstances when your enemy is already defeated?

Keep your foot on the devil's neck. You don't have to struggle. Just keep your big foot on his neck. His days are numbered.

Jesse's Daughter Jodi's Four-Leaf Salad with Garlic Balsamic Vinaigrette

Salad
½ head red leaf lettuce
1 head boston lettuce
½ head curly-q lettuce
½ head raddiccio
2 or 3 handfuls red seedless grapes
2 or 3 handfuls chopped walnuts
3 handfuls or to taste crumbled blue cheese
    (or goat cheese)
1 or 2 handfuls dried cranberries
sunflower seeds (optional for crunchiness)

Wash, dry and tear up lettuce. Pour on a generous amount of dressing and hand toss until all the lettuce is covered. Add blue cheese, walnuts, dried cranberries, sunflower seeds and grapes. Hand toss again until salad is covered in dressing. Add more dressing if needed. Chill for 5 minutes to allow dressing to permeate salad. Serve.

Jodi says, "Dad loves it!"

Dressing
1 cup olive oil
1 or 2 "swigs" balsamic vinaigrette
2-3 garlic quarters
½ handful shallots, chopped
generous amount black pepper
moderate amount thyme
Anything else you think would taste good—
rosemary, K Paul's vegetable seasoning mix or any
Cajun vegetable seasoning mix.

If you're using your good seasonings croquet,
fill vinegar to waterline, oil to oil line (oil is somewhere over a cup or so; vinegar is a few good swigs).
Add garlic and shallots, then seasonings. Shake well
and serve. Olive oil solidifies when refrigerated,
so make sure to take dressing out of fridge about 5
minutes before preparing salad in order to allow oil to
become liquid.

Great Variations of the same salad:
Fresh Blueberries and Goat Cheese (omit grapes
   and blue cheese)
Dried Blueberries, Sugared Pecans and Goat Cheese
   (omit cranberries, walnuts and blue cheese)
Chopped Greek Olives and Crumbled Feta Cheese
   (omit grapes, cranberries and blue cheese)

2

Dracula and Pleading the Blood

After my mamma and daddy got saved when I was little, they didn't want my brother and I to watch television anymore. Instead they got us those Bible storybooks and that kind of stuff. They said, "We want you to read the Word of God."

Well, one night I sneaked out to watch a program, and I saw *Dracula,* with Bella Lagosi, you know. Ahhhhhhhhhhh, he was scary! I was eight years old, and I freaked out. I mean it was scary stuff. I came back home that night, and every time I was about to fall asleep, I'd remember something from the movie and get freaked out. Every time I closed my eyes, I'd see that bat. I'd just see that bat, and it scared me.

I remembered that Mamma had told me, "If you ever get scared, boy, just say the name of Jesus." I remembered that as I was freaking out over that bat.

So I said, "Jesus, Jesus, Jesus, Jesus, Jesus, Jesus, Jesus, Jesus, Jesus, Jesus, Jesus."

I closed my eyes, and that bat came back. Man, I said "Jesus" all over the place! I said it so much my brother asked, "What's the matter with you?"

"Wayne," I said, "every time I close my eyes I see Dracula."

"You been watching television?" Wayne asked.

"Yeah, man," I said.

"Wow, what was the picture about?"

"The guy sucks blood like you've never seen," I told him. "He's going to kill both of us tonight. It's going to happen, Wayne. I just want to let you know that."

Then I closed my eyes again and said, "Jesus, Jesus, Jesus." I mean, I must have said that for forty minutes: "Jesus, Jesus, Jesus, Jesus, Jesus, Jesus, Jesus, Jesus."

Finally Wayne said, "Shut up, man! I can't even sleep."

"Jesus, Jesus, Jesus, Jesus."

"I'm gonna tell Mamma."

"No, no, no. Jesus, Jesus."

Finally, Wayne hollered out, "Mamma, Jesse watched *Dracula,* and he's saying, 'Jesus, Jesus, Jesus, Jesus, Jesus.' I can't sleep!"

Mamma came in and said, "You been watching *Dracula*, boy?"

"Mamma, every time I close my eyes, I see that bat," I said.

"Well, plead the blood," she said.

"Noooooo! He likes blood! We ain't messing with no blood. Ohhh, nooo, forget the blood—huh-uh. I ain't dealing with blood. This guy *likes* blood."

About that time my daddy came in from work, and I told him about Dracula. "Daddy, Dracula's coming, and he's going to kill us all!"

I'll never forget my daddy. He picked me up by my T-shirt. I was a little fellow. He said, "Do you think I'm more powerful than Dracula?" Then he looked at me and said, "Boy, Jesus is in this house, and so am I. And Mamma is too."

"Well, Daddy, that took care of it when you said Mamma is too," I said.

"Now go to sleep," he said.

"I ain't messing with Dracula no more," I said. And I fell off to sleep.

That night I learned who was more powerful. Daddy told me Jesus was with him and Mamma and the three of them weren't going to let anybody mess with

me. That made me feel safe, because I knew Dracula or anything else that was evil couldn't get to me.

The devil is like that Dracula I watched on TV. He roams around like a roaring lion trying to attack people. (1 Peter 5:8.) But as long as you've got Jesus, you know the devil can't get to you. The devil may be able to roar, but he can't bite you because Jesus is on your side! The devil's roars are always a false alarm.

abdominal, detestable, horrible.
*"If you don get a hair cut you gone to look like de **abdominal** snowman."*

3

FRED AND THE OUTHOUSE

I'll never forget this one incident as long as I live. It happened when I was about five-and-a-half years old. Back then my family lived down in a place called Sheffield Lane. We lived in the back of the town by the Mississippi River levee. That was where my brother Wayne and I would play.

In that same neighborhood was a kid Wayne and I used to play with. But this kid was an abused child, because both his parents were alcoholics and they would neglect him sometimes. This boy's name was Fred, and Fred was a tough kid. At the age of six Fred would smoke cigars, and that freaked me out. I'd say, "Wow, man! Fred's smoking."

"Want a hit?" Fred would ask, offering me his cigar.

"No, no, no," I would say.

Fred's parents didn't much care what Fred did. I saw his father fall drunk on the porch many times. His mamma too. The police would go down there, pick up the kids and keep them for about three weeks, but eventually they'd give them back.

So Fred was a tough kid. In fact, he once took a butter knife and stabbed one of my friends in the back with it. An ambulance had to come pick up my friend. That made me mad.

"We're going to whip Fred," I told my brother.

"Okay," my brother agreed. "Where are we gonna whip him at?"

Well, I had a plan to get even with Fred.

Back then we didn't have an inside toilet. We had an outside toilet called a "three-holer." There was the daddy holer, the mamma holer and the baby holer—a three-holer toilet. You were a hotshot if you had a three-holer.

I told my brother how I was going to get even with Fred. I said, "I'm going to lure Fred into that outhouse. You get there first and wait behind the door. Then when I open the door and he comes in, you just hit him. After you hit him, I'll throw him down the hole."

Oh, I was a bad kid. Remember, I was about five-and-a half years old when this happened.

"I done had enough of Fred," I said. "Fred stabbed our friend, and we're gonna bust him today."

Well, sure enough, before long ol' Fred came over, smoking his cigar. I'll never forget it. I said, "Hey, Fred, come here."

"What d'ya want?" Fred asked.

"Come here," I said. "I want to tell you something. I got something to show you in the outhouse too. Come see."

"There ain't nothing in there I want to see," Fred said.

"Just come on," I said.

Now, Wayne was in the outhouse, waiting behind the door, and I was tricking Fred into coming in there. Boy, when he walked through that door, *boom!* Wayne hit him! And when Wayne hit him, I hit him too. I yelled, "You stabbed my friend!" And we started to beat him up.

Well, my plan was to throw Fred down one of those holes. I was trying to throw him in, but all I had gotten in so far was his head. But I was sure trying to get the rest of him down there.

He was going, "Ahhhhhhhhhhhhhhhhhhhhhhh!"

I was trying to get even with Fred for stabbing my friend with a butter knife. I was sticking up for my

friend. Here I was five-and-a-half years old, and that's how I was going to get even.

Fred was screaming at the top of his lungs. We were trying to stuff him down that hole—but the problem was I had his head in one hole and his legs in another, and there was something in between. I couldn't get him all the way in. I wanted to cut him in half and drop both halves in there.

Just then I heard Fred's daddy coming after us. I heard him, and I got so scared I left Fred hanging in the holes and started to run. Wayne ran too.

Fred came out crying, "Ohhhhhhhhh!" And his daddy ran up, yelling, "Hey! I ought to kill you."

Now, I was just a little guy, and when that big man said something about killing us, I froze. Wayne was yelling, "Run, Jesse, run!" But I was scared frozen.

Fred's dad was drunk, and he was holding a big Stillson wrench. Anybody know what I'm talking about? He had a big monkey wrench, an oil field wrench. And he was holding that wrench, saying, "I'll kill you, boy!"

So I was standing there frozen, and Wayne was still screaming, "Run! *Run!*" Wayne was running. But I was just standing there with this guy and his wrench

coming at me. He got right up close and said, "I'll beat your brains out!"

All of a sudden I heard something go, *Kukukkk!* I turned around, and there was my mamma, standing in the doorway with a .22-caliber rifle pointed at that man's head.

"You touch my boy, and I'll kill you," she told that man.

As soon as she said that, I'm telling you, boldness came up in me. I had so much boldness all of a sudden, I just looked at that man and said, "Yeah, you want some of me? Come on, man. I'll whip your son and whip you too. Mess with me!" Five-and-half years old! I had so much boldness that I yelled, "Shoot him, Mamma!"

Mamma said, "Shut up, Jesse! *Shut up!*" Then she turned back to the man and repeated, "You touch my boy, and I'll kill ya!" By that time my daddy had come out. He saw my mamma with a .22, he saw the guy with a wrench and he saw me going, "Come on, Jack."

My daddy saw all that and started to talk my mother out of it. Her name was Velma, but daddy called her Vel. He said, "Vel! Don't kill that man."

That man looked at my daddy and said, "You think she would?"

My daddy told that man, "I live with this woman, and I know her. She *will* kill you if you touch that boy!"

Mamma had that rifle with seventeen shots pointed right at the man's head. Boy, did I have boldness!

Daddy called to my mamma, "Mamma, put the gun down."

Daddy was trying to get people saved; Mamma was trying to kill them.

She answered my daddy, "Paul, I haven't crucified my flesh yet. You believe in raising the dead, right? Well, we'll see how much power you've got. I'll bust him in a second if he touches Jesse."

That man dropped the wrench and backed away—very, very slowly.

I knew that man had been scared, and that had made me even more bold. As long as my mamma was backing me up, I had boldness. Why did I have boldness? Because there was somebody behind me with a gun! I had someone protecting me.

Let me tell you something. The devil may be coming at you with a wrench, brother or sister, ready to bust your head open. You may have done something to make him mad, and he just doesn't like it. Maybe you did something wrong, or maybe you did something right. The devil doesn't care. He comes to steal, kill and destroy. (John 10:10.)

Well, with God on your side, you can look over at Jesus and hear Him say, "Come here, kid!" It's Him saying, "You touch that kid, and I'll blow your head off! You don't touch that kid! That's My boy." Or, "That's My girl." Glory to God. Hallelujah! You're Jesus' kid, and He sticks up for you just like my mamma did with that gun.

Knowing that produces boldness inside you!

Jesse's Sister-in-Law Christine's Banana Pudding

- 1 ½ cups sugar
- 3 heaping tablespoons flour
- 3 eggs
- ¼ teaspoon vanilla flavoring
- 2 ½ cups milk
- ½ stick of butter
- 2 boxes of vanilla wafers
- 8 large bananas

In an oblong baking dish, layer the wafers and bananas, ending with wafers as the top layer.

Mix dry ingredients well. Beat eggs and mix in milk. Mix dry ingredients and egg-and-milk mixture with a wire whisk. In a large saucepan, cook pudding mixture over low heat, stirring constantly with a wire whisk while cooking until it starts to thicken. Remove from heat. Pour pudding over wafers and bananas.

This dessert is best eaten while it is still warm.

4

Fight at
the Airport

I was in Pittsburgh, Pennsylvania, some years ago waiting to catch a plane. As I sat there, I saw a woman coming over to board a commuter flight. In Pittsburgh you have to check in before you board the airplane. They don't care if you've got a boarding pass or not; it doesn't make any difference—you've got to check in.

There are at least twenty-five commuter planes going out of there all the time.

Well, this woman got into line, and I noticed her carry-on items. Now, why is it that women have to carry thirty-nine bags on their body when they get onto a plane? Have you ever noticed that? They've got one strapped across their shoulder, one hung from the neck, two on the arm and so on. They walk all slanted because of these bags hanging off them.

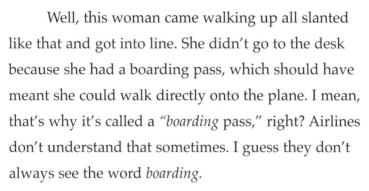

Well, this woman came walking up all slanted like that and got into line. She didn't go to the desk because she had a boarding pass, which should have meant she could walk directly onto the plane. I mean, that's why it's called a *"boarding* pass," right? Airlines don't understand that sometimes. I guess they don't always see the word *boarding*.

Well, this woman came walking up with all of her bags, and I could tell she was tired. She walked up to the man and handed him her boarding pass so she could get on the plane. The man took one look at her and said, "Excuse me, ma'am. Ah, have you checked in at the gate?"

Now, the gate was only about a stone's throw away, because this was a commuter flight. It was only a little bitty flight.

"Well, no," she told him, "but I have my seating assignment." The seating assignment was listed on the boarding pass.

"Well, I'm sorry," he said. "You'll have to check in at the gate."

By this time there were a bunch of people in line behind her. She had been standing there for a while before he came over and asked her that question.

"You mean to tell me I have to go over there and check in?" she said, pointing to the desk. "I have a boarding pass," she continued. "You people sent me a boarding pass, which means I can board the plane. I already have my seat selected. Here's the seat number," she said, holding the boarding pass up to the man.

"I'm sorry, ma'am," he said, "but everybody's got boarding passes. You've got to check in first at the gate."

This did *not* make that lady happy. She said, "Well, I am not going to! I've carried these bags all over this airport, and I'm not going over to that gate."

"Well, I'm sorry ma'am, but you can't get on the plane."

"What do you mean I can't get on the plane?" she snapped.

"Well, you've got to check in at the gate first." He said, "In fact, you're ten minutes late now, and we've given up your seat."

"No, you haven't!" she said. She was getting fired up now, boy.

"Oh, yes, ma'am, we have," he said.

And, man, I saw it. I saw the devil take that woman. And I'll be honest, I was half mad at the man myself. I said to myself, *Well, at least I'm not sinning.*

I'll just watch her sin awhile. Bless God, I was mad at
him too!

At about that time she took one of those bags
off her back. She was getting serious. Then she started
taking the other bags off, and she said, "I'm not carrying these bags anymore." And she dropped them right
in front of the exit.

He said, "Now, ma'am, you've got to move
your bags."

"I don't have to move *blubbbblldootttdodotodot!*"
she shouted.

There was no interpreter present, but everybody
understood what the woman said. Man, I saw her get
hot. She was a very elegant lady, about forty-five. She
had really nice jewelry, nice clothes and those were
nice bags she was dragging. I know it was tough.

"Well, ma'am," he said, "you're just going to
have to get in another line."

"I'm not getting out of line; I'm going to get in
your face!" she said.

Standing next to me was a guy who had been
watching the whole thing as well. When she said that,
we both backed up against the wall. I'll never forget
that. If you ever go to Pittsburgh and you go to gate

24, you'll know what I'm talking about. Our backs were up against that wall.

As soon as she said she was going to get in that man's face, she reared back and hit that guy. *Wham!* She just socked him in the eye.

The man next to me said, "Did you see that?"

I muttered, "Uh-huh."

Then she turned around and cussed everybody out. Man, she cussed out everybody in the line. And believe me, everybody backed away then. When she was done with the people in line, she turned back to the man at the desk and cried, "You go get that pass now! I'm getting on that blankety-blank plane!"

She never did get that pass. Just then two uniformed policemen came up to get her. And just as they were coming, someone from the line yelled, "Hey, boys, you better have some shields! This woman will scratch your eyes out."

She was mad.

While all this was going on, I was up against the wall, saying to myself, *Hit him on the other side.* There isn't any use lying to you. I was thinking that. That's the truth.

They dragged that woman off to jail. I mean, they literally dragged her out of there. Her bags were

still on the floor where she left them. After she left, the man started fixing himself up, but he had a puffy eye where she'd busted him. She hit him good.

By the time we were supposed to board the plane, not one of us made a move. We were all in shock after what we had just witnessed. But after I got on the plane, I heard the Lord say to me, *You could have at least prayed.*

He was right. What I should have done was say, "I rebuke this devil in Jesus' name." But I didn't want a high heel stuck in my head. But that's what I should've done. I should've rebuked the devil for influencing the woman to hit that guy.

Did you know that you have the power to do that? You have spiritual authority over circumstances. So you don't have to be a spectator like I was when something terrible is happening—you can do something about it. I could've done something right then.

You see, Jesus gave us all authority over the works of evil, and that incident in the airport was a work of evil. Jesus told us that He gave us authority to trample on serpents and scorpions. (Luke 10:19.) That means we don't have to let the devil run all over us or anybody else. We can pray about it and rebuke the devil. We have that authority!

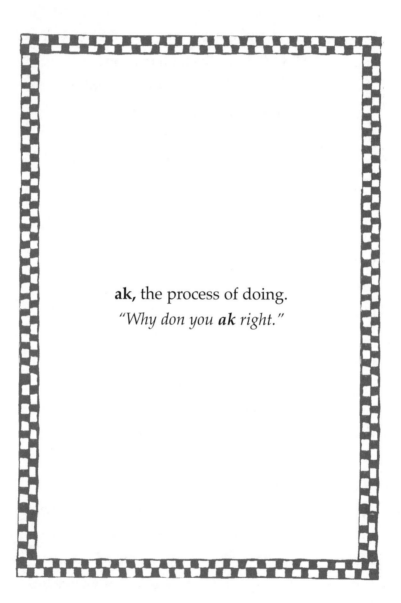

ak, the process of doing.
*"Why don you **ak** right."*

5

DiETS STiNK

I saw a guy in the airport the other day, and he was wearing Western clothes. From the back he looked like a little bitty guy, but when he turned around—oh boy—in front it was like a crane swinging around. He had a gut, man! I mean, his belly was full. He must've had on jeans with a 30-inch waist, and they were skintight. I don't know how he did it, but he had gotten them on under that belly! He must've had trouble just breathing!

Now, what did he need in his life? A diet? No. Diets don't work. Why? Because they have a terrible name: diet. *Die*—t. That's not good. The minute you think about going on a diet, your body sends signals to itself that say, *Famine! Famine! Eat! Eat! Eat! Store! Store! Store it in the back where no one can see it! Store! Store! Eat! Don't say the word* diet.

Here's another word your body doesn't want to hear: fast. When you think about fasting, your body says, *No! Eat—hurry!* Your body says, *Famine is coming! It's cutting us off!*

Now, when you feed your body too much, do you know what your body says? Your body starts thinking, *Boy, we must have some trouble ahead. Store it up! There must be some hard times a-comin', Jack. He wouldn't put this much in here otherwise. I don't know what's going on, but I guarantee you one thing—ooooh Lord! recession is coming. Build fat! There ain't no use to burn it. Slow the metabolism down. Don't burn this stuff, because it's going to get bad in here, Jack.*

That's exactly what your body is saying when you're overeating, because it wonders why you would do that. It sends you a signal when it's had enough. It's called a little burp. Do we listen? No, because we don't eat to get full. We eat because it tastes good.

We say, "I think I'll have another little bite there. And another little bite there." After a while the body is going, *Hey! We're choking down here, man!* In fact, it doesn't know what to do, so it says, *Man, I can't move. Let's get sleepy. Your body says, Hey, I can't handle this. Shut him down. If he doesn't shut his mouth, he'll kill us. Zzzzzzzzzzz.*

Is that true? Oh, yeah. But once you regulate it and you give it what it needs, you never have to

worry about fat anymore. Yeah, but some of you say, "Oh, I can't do better, Jesse. I've tried all of those diets. You know, my weight problem is in the genes." Yeah, your problem is in your jeans all right, and it's trying to bust out over the sides, too!

Have you ever seen women wearing jeans with fat hanging over the top? You say, "How come you don't stuff that in somewhere?"

And they say, "I tried to put it in, but it pops right back out!"

The same thing happens with men. But what they do is pull their fat up above their belts, and then they think they're not fat. If they didn't pull the fat up above their belts, then they'd have to change pants sizes. So instead they say, "What I'm going to do is put my pants under that belly. I wear pants with a 32-inch waist, but I have a 94-inch belly. Oh, no! I'm not buying pants any bigger than this! You can forget that, Jack! Just put them underneath the fat. *Way* underneath!"

But you can't let your body boss you around like that. You've got to tell *it* what to do, not let it tell *you* what to do. No, you just say, "Body, you're going to do what I tell you to do!" See, quit being dictated by the flesh, by what the appetite says. I'm not saying it's easy. It's not. If it were easy, everybody would do

it, and everybody would be as skinny as they wanted to be.

You can eat all you like if you want, but it's not going to be helpful to you. Listen to what Paul says about that in the Bible: **"Everything is permissible for me"—but not everything is beneficial. "Everything is permissible for me"—but I will not be mastered by anything.** (1 Cor. 6:12 NIV).

This principle can be applied to eating as well as other appetites we have. The very next thing Paul says is about food and the stomach. He's telling us that we should keep our appetites under control so we don't have to go on a diet or, worse yet, "hide" all that fat up above our jeans.

Jesse's Brother-in-Law Rickey's Boiled Crawfish

40–45	pounds live crawfish
2–2½	boxes salt (iodine-free salt)
6	bags of Zatarain's Crab Boil
1	small bottle of liquid Zatarain's Crab Boil
2	pounds of small red potatoes, quartered
6	onions
12	lemons, quartered
3	bulbs garlic
12	small cobs of corn

You will need an outside burner to cook on. You will also need a 30-40 gallon pot with a colander to cook the crawfish in.

In a large washtub, wash crawfish and remove the dead ones. In the 30-gallon pot, add 15 gallons of cold water (the pot should be half full). Add the potatoes, onions, lemons, garlic and the 6 bags of Zatarain's Crab Boil. Bring to a boil, and simmer for 10-12 minutes. This will cook the potatoes and season the water. Add the live crawfish and corn. When the water begins to boil again, add 2 boxes of salt. Stir thoroughly, being careful not to break the crab boil bags. Continue boiling for 3–5 minutes. Turn off heat and add 1 small bottle of liquid crab boil. Stir thoroughly.

If you like your crawfish extra spicy, you can add about 4–6 ounces of cayenne pepper, liquid or powder, at this time.

Let the crawfish soak for 5–8 minutes. Taste for saltiness. If it is not salty enough, add $\frac{1}{2}$ box of salt to water and stir thoroughly. Let the crawfish continue to soak in the water for an additional 2–3 minutes. Take another sample taste. Mixture should be just about the right saltiness. If not, allow the crawfish to soak in the water for 2–3 minutes longer.

Promptly remove colander, lifting crawfish from the water. This stops the cooking process. Pour drained crawfish into another container, removing the crab boil bags and being careful not to break them. You can also remove the potatoes, corn, onions and garlic at this time.

Serve crawfish on large platters, or just pour onto a paper-covered table.

6

ReBuKiNg BEER PigS

Before Jesus became a part of my life, I drank a lot. I'd down a bottle of whiskey every day as part of my normal routine. My two favorites were scotch and tequila. I put tequila in my breakfast cereal with the milk in the morning, and most days I probably ate more worms at the bottom of a tequila bottle than the earliest bird on your block. I drank so much scotch that I could have set a city on fire with my breath and the strike of a match. In fact, a doctor told me that I'd have cirrhosis of the liver and die before I hit twenty-five if I didn't stop drinking.

Thank God, on Labor Day weekend in 1974, the Lord came into my life and supernaturally set me free from drugs and alcohol. I'm living today because of His saving grace. But just to give you an example about how strong temptation can be, I'll tell you what happened to me several years ago in Dallas.

Now, I'd been a preacher for a lot of years.
I was going to preach to the students at Christ for
the Nations Bible School in Dallas. They had sent a
student to pick me up from the airport. So when this
young man picked me up, he was excited to meet me.
He said, "Oh, Brother Jesse, I'm so excited to have the
opportunity and honor to pick you up. I hope I'm not
talking too much."

I said, "No, no, you're not talking too much.
That's fine."

After that he looked at me and said, "Man, you're
sure shorter in person than you are on television!"

"Now you're talking too much!" I said.

Anyway, we were laughing and talking and
getting along great while driving back from the
airport. Now, this young guy kept giving me all these
compliments. And I'm not the kind of person who
takes compliments too well. So I just kept saying,
"Well, thank you. Thank you," and thinking, *Let's get
on to something else. We don't need to talk about me so
much. Let's just go on.*

So we were driving down the interstate, and
we started passing these billboards on the side of the
road. Well, we passed this one huge billboard that
was advertising beer. It caught my attention because

it had a literal waterfall coming out of the sign. Real
water gushed out of this beautiful picture, and it had a
slogan about how refreshing the beer was.

Now, I hate the taste of beer. I always had. And
you know, I hadn't even thought about drinking in
years, but for some reason, as I was looking at that
waterfall, my mouth started to water. And my mind
started to wander. I mean, I'm saved, full of the Holy
Ghost and was on my way to preach a meeting. But I
saw this sign, and listen, I began to salivate! I entertained
the thoughts for a bit until, all of a sudden, I caught
myself. I realized what I was doing. But the temptation was so strong that I just couldn't keep it to myself.

"I rebuke you, in Jesus name!" I hollered.

The kid in the car slammed on the brakes and
looked at me with eyes as big as saucers.

"Oh, I'm sorry! Brother Jesse, what did I do?"

"You didn't do anything!"

He just looked at me, scared and not knowing
what to think.

"I was rebuking the flesh. I used to drink a lot, and
my body tried to make me remember the trash it used
to do. And I saw that sign and rebuked temptation!"

He just nodded. He looked straight ahead and
stayed that way as he nervously started back towards

campus. He never said another thing the rest of the way. I don't know what he told his friends about the crazy preacher who hollers at billboards, but I can tell you this—that was one mind-boggling temptation that got stopped dead in its tracks that day! There's something about confronting temptation head-on and embarrassing yourself that makes you not actually follow through with it. It brings it right out in the open.

You see, your body is not saved. I don't care how saved *you* are—your body is not. That's why I had to take care of that problem right then when it happened. Boy or no boy, I had to bind up that devil right then. And that's how you've got to treat temptation. You don't let it get comfortable with you. You've got to deal with it the minute it starts getting bad. The sooner you deal with temptation, the less hold it has on you.

Don't wait until your problem becomes the size of a full-grown tree; deal with it while it's still a tiny shoot or small seed. When the devil first sends you a temptation, resist it right away while it's easy to take care of. If you keep thinking about the temptation, it'll grow up. Don't let your temptations grow up. Pull them up at the root!

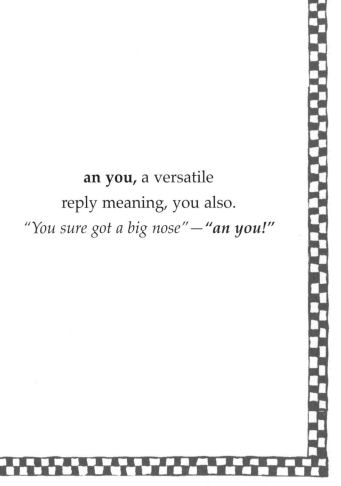

an you, a versatile
reply meaning, you also.
*"You sure got a big nose"—**"an you!"***

7

EMBaRRaSSiNg SiN ON aN AirPLaNE

I've learned to attack sin instead of waiting for sin to attack me. I remember this one time when I walked onto a plane, found my seat and was minding my own business. I was just sitting there, waiting for the plane to take off. In fact, I wasn't even paying attention to anyone, because I was reading a newspaper. So I was just sitting in my seat, reading a newspaper, waiting for the plane to take off.

All of a sudden this beautiful, foxy mamma—I'm not talking about no dog now—comes up to me. This was a good-looking woman! Now, I've got my head in the paper, and there are several men and a couple of ladies sitting around me. And I noticed this woman when she walked up to my row and stopped. You know, when you see somebody standing right in front of you, you look up. I was in the aisle seat, so I

thought she had a window seat in my row or something like that.

But instead of going to her seat, the woman said to me, "Aren't you glad that I'm sitting by you?"

I couldn't believe she said that! I looked at that beautiful woman and said, "Ma'am?" That's all I could say because she kind of took me by surprise.

So she said again, "Aren't you glad that I'm sitting by you today? Whooooo! Aren't you glad?"

Well, I'm not going to be sad. No. I'm not going to say that I was sad she was sitting next to me. That would be rude.

"Yes, ma'am," I said. "Ah, is this your window seat?"

She didn't even answer my question. She just jumped in, saying, "I'll tell you what. I really like your hair."

When she said that, I started hearing these noises behind me, "Wahhhh haaaaa ahhhh. Waaaaaaaaaah." It was these two men carrying on. You know how men are. They get stupid. I mean their hormones start kicking in, you know. Once a guy's hormones take over, he doesn't know what's going on anymore.

The woman was standing there, and I just looked at her.

She said, "We could make beautiful music together." She said this out loud in front of everybody! Then she said, "Where are you going?"

Now that's a dumb question: "Where are you going?" I mean, we're on the same plane! I'm going the same place she's going—where else?

That's exactly what I told her too. I said, "Same place you're going."

So then she said, "What are you doing? Listen, why don't we just go somewhere?" She actually said this! You know, this woman was laying it on thick right there in the aisle.

When she said that, those men just cut loose. They started howling, "Whooo, ouhhhhhh, wowww-wwwww!" Everybody around us could hear them, saying, "Whoaaaa, man!"

But I was just sitting there looking at her. *Heh, heh, heh,* I thought to myself. I started smiling, because I knew what I was going to do.

"What do you do?" she asked me.

Well, I just looked at her really good, boy. Meanwhile, everybody was freaking out. I mean, especially those guys behind me. They were losing it, you know. Even the gray hair on their chests were starting to curl up. Some of those old boys were trying

to cover their bald heads. They were just getting into it, you know, because she was a pretty lady. And she was a nice person as far as I knew.

So I just looked at her and smiled.

She said, "You know, we could just have such a wonderful time together." And while she was saying that she started patting me on the hand.

I just smiled at her. And then as loud as I could—I mean, I didn't even wait to get out of my seat—I sat right there in the seat and yelled, "Whore of Babylon! *Whore of Babylon!* WHORE OF BABYLON!"

She screamed, "Ahhhhhhhhh!" She didn't know what to do.

I heard one of the men say, "Where's Babylon?" He wanted to know where Babylon was! This woman had gotten the socks embarrassed off her, and this guy was trying to figure out where Babylon was.

Well, when I said that, it shut everything down. That woman certainly didn't sit by me! In fact, she ran to the back of the plane and sat down. She was too embarrassed to sit with me.

Why did I say that to her? Let me tell you something. You'd better embarrass sin. If you don't embarrass sin, sin will embarrass you. But if you embarrass sin, it will never embarrass you. The more you let it, the more sin will embarrass you. That's why I told that woman off.

When you get into a situation and it looks like sin can come in, you'd better kick it out. You can't just kick sin out lightly either. You've got to be tough with it. Treat it like Jesus did when He told the devil, "Get behind me, Satan!" (Luke 4:8.) Get tough with sin. You won't regret it. I like to think of it this way: Sin will keep you longer than you want to stay and charge you more than you want to pay.

Jesse's Son-in-Law Eddie's Mother's Bread Pudding

    3 loaves stale french bread
    1 can condensed milk
    1 dozen eggs
    1 gallon milk
    1 stick butter
    2 cups sugar
    1 tablespoon vanilla

Break the bread apart in a large soup pot until there are no big chunks. Add butter and condensed milk. Separate the eggs, and place whites in a separate bowl to be used for the meringue. Add the yolks to the mixture. Add the sugar, and start pouring in the milk until the bread becomes saturated. You will use about ¾ of the gallon of milk. Stir mixture. Add vanilla and mix well. Add more sugar or vanilla to taste. In a 9x13 cake pan, pour in the bread pudding and smooth out. Bake in a 375° oven for 1 to 1 ½ hours. Check after 1 hour. Using a knife, pierce the bread pudding; if the knife comes out doughy, keep baking. Repeat process until the knife comes out clean. When it is done, remove, but do not turn off oven.

Meringue
1 dozen egg whites
½ cup sugar
1 teaspoon cream of tartar
pinch of salt

To egg whites, add salt, sugar and cream of tartar. Mix with mixer. Mixture will become fluffy. When fluffy, taste. If it is not sweet, add more sugar. Continue to mix until meringue becomes thick and you can make peaks. Spread the mixture on top of the bread pudding, making peaks with a spoon. Bake again for 10 minutes at 325° until peaks brown. Watch closely to make sure it does not burn. Take out and let cool before serving. After cooling to room temperature, keep refrigerated.

8

ATTack of THE ViENNa SausaGE

Healing has been a part of my life for a long time. Once I got the revelation on walking in health, I've been free from sickness ever since. I've had some great opportunities to get sick, but I've resisted every one of them. I remember this one time especially.

Cathy was out of town, and I had the whole house to myself. That meant that I had to do all the cooking. Now, Cathy doesn't cook when she is home. We have pots and pans that are all clean. We have china and crystal that are untouched. You ought to see them because that's all you can do—just see them.

So when I got hungry, I had to get creative. I had to look around for something that was ready to eat, and the only thing I could find was a can of Vienna sausages in the pantry. I hadn't eaten Vienna sausages in ten years. Ten years is a long time.

Now, you can tell that Vienna sausages are really, really healthy. You can tell that just by looking at the stuff. It's got all that Vienna jelly all over it. I tried to take the jelly stuff off, but it wouldn't come off. It's really slippery, but I finally got one of those suckers out of there and looked at it. I thought to myself, *I didn't like this stuff ten years ago, and I still don't like it.*

I ate that one Vienna sausage and threw the rest of them away.

Well, a long time later I was getting ready to go to bed. You see, I don't go to bed until the early morning hours, around 1 or 2 A.M. I'm a night person. So at about one in the morning, I got ready for bed and started to pray. I said, "Lord, I just thank You for today," before I went to bed.

God said, *You might want to pray a little longer.*

"No, I think I'm going on to bed, Jesus." I said.

Well, when I got into bed, the bed started moving on me. It really felt strange. I couldn't handle that, so I went into the bathroom. Now, in the bathroom there's this stained glass thing over the bathtub. And when I looked at the stained glass, it started moving too. First the bed was moving, and then the stained glass was moving too.

I felt like I was dying. I haven't felt that bad in fifteen years. I mean, I couldn't lie down, I was panting and I was almost passing out. Sweat broke out all over my body, and the devil started telling me, *This is it, Jack. You're going to die with a Vienna sausage in your mouth!*

"That's a lie," I told him. I had to start fighting the devil to keep my healing. Then it dawned on me to turn to Jesus! I turned to Jesus on the inside of me and started to pray. I laid hands on myself and tried to pray between gulps of air: "Jesus—*gasp*—heal—*gasp*—my—*gasp*—bo—*gasp*—dy!"

And do you know what? I began to breathe better. Healing came to my body. In fact, I felt so good I went jogging just to prove to the devil that I was healed. And when I came back, do you know what the Lord said to me? He said, *Go read what that can of Vienna sausages says.*

I found out after checking the expiration date that the can of sausages really *was* over ten years old, and it was my own dumb fault for eating them in the first place. But God healed me anyway.

You see, God will heal us when we make mistakes. He just wants you to be in health. God told us that it's His will that we prosper in all things and

be in health. (3 John 2.) God is on our side. He doesn't want us to be sick or suffer.

That's why Jesus healed me that night. After that He told me, *The next time you eat something, read the label first. And don't eat anything in your pantry. It's all old!*

aw, an expression of
doubt or amazement.
*"Ah caught a 30 lb. green trout
last week"* — *"Aw"*

9

TRaSH GUMBO

I was preaching at a meeting once, when afterward this lady came up to me and said, "Brother Jesse, I'm going to cook you the best gumbo you'll ever eat in your life."

Now, I very seldom ever go to people's homes and eat. It's not that I'm unfriendly; I'm a very friendly man. But if I did that, then I'd have to go eat everywhere. You understand? And I'd weigh five thousand pounds. So I hardly ever go to people's homes to eat dinner.

But this woman said she was going to make me the best gumbo I'd ever eaten, and I thought, *Honey, you've got a long way to go!* I thought that because this woman wasn't even from Louisiana. Now, to make good gumbo, you've got to be from Louisiana, especially Southern Louisiana, where people *know* how to make gumbo.

You know, some people think a gumbo is just a chicken diving into a pot and then jumping right back out. Well, that's nothing more than plain old boiled chicken. That's not gumbo.

Well, I went over to this woman's home, met her husband and kids and sat down with the family for dinner. Now, this woman's husband wasn't saved, so he just kind of sat there, checking me out. He knew I was a preacher and probably thought I wanted an offering or something.

The kids really liked me, though. They kept saying, "Brother Jesse, we're so glad you came over to our house."

Finally, after all the cooking was done, the woman brought the gumbo in and put it on the table in front of me. She brought it right to me. Now, I looked at that gumbo, and I could tell right away that it was "El Trasho." I could tell just by looking at it. I knew it was bad—I just knew it! So I thought, *Well, I'm going to eat this stuff because Mamma always said, "Eat whatever is set before you." And if this woman asks me how it is, I'm going to lie like a dog. That's what I'm going to do.*

I said to myself, *I'm going to tell a little white lie.*

But the Lord heard that and said, *No lies are white, Jesse. You be honest about the gumbo.*

I told the Lord, *That's easy for You to say. I'm the one down here at this table. I've got to eat this trash, You understand. You're up in heaven saying, "Suffer." I don't want to eat this stuff!*

Anyway, she brought the gumbo right over to me, and then everybody just sat there looking at me to see what I was going to do. So with everybody watching, I picked up the spoon—one of those big spoons, you see. It was a gumbo spoon, so it was bigger than a normal spoon. And I noticed that the husband was looking at me funny. He wasn't tasting the gumbo. I mean, he wasn't just looking—he was staring!

Now, the two kids weren't eating anything either. They were just sitting there looking at me, too. I'm not exaggerating a bit. That whole family was just staring at me, and I was thinking, *God, what am I supposed to do?* I guess they thought that, because I am a Cajun, I was going to test this gumbo properly.

What else could I do? I took this big spoonful of gumbo and put it in my mouth. *Arhguhhhhhhh. Awwwwwwwwwwghhhh.* Son, I mean, it was bad! *Whoooooo,* it was trash. I mean, bad. Bad. *Major* bad! You could've killed plants with it!

So I sat there going, "Ohhhh."

And the woman asked, "Well, how do you like it, Brother Jesse?"

My mind told me, *Lie, lie, lie.* And the Lord said, *Don't you lie. You tell her the truth.* So I started praying, *Rapture! Get me out of here. Get me out of here. Rapture! Now!*

I didn't want to say anything. I mean, I'm not a rude man. If I told her the gumbo was bad, to me it would be rude. So I was just sitting there with my spoon in my hand, and her husband was looking at me with his spoon in his hand. He hadn't even touched it yet! Neither had the kids! They were all still just looking at me.

So the lady asked again, "Well, how do you like it, Brother Jesse?"

I said, "Well, Ma'am...." *God,* I thought, *I've got to be honest.*

"Ma'am, this is trash."

I had to tell her the truth. And as soon as I did, her husband threw down his spoon and said, "Now I know you're a man of God. I *know* you are!" It shocked me.

And the kids dropped their spoons too.

The man said, "Honey, this is trash! We've been eating it for years. Please, don't ever make this again. Ever. Never. Never. It's trash!"

And the kids started up, "Mamma, we didn't want to hurt your feelings, but please never cook it again."

I looked over in the corner, and I could see the dog going, *Thank You, Jesus. I ain't got to eat this junk again either.*

That man told me he had had preachers come over, eat that junk and lie like a dog. He said, "We knew it was no good. You're the first man who ever told us the truth. That's why I believe you're a man of God."

That man got saved two weeks later because of that dumb old, trashy gumbo. But I had to be honest about it. I had to call it what it was—junk.

That's why you have to know the voice of the Holy Spirit. You can be in situations in which you think you should say the polite thing, but it's not always the right thing. You've got to say the right thing even if it's not the polite thing. Knowing the difference is a matter of trusting the promptings of the Holy Spirit.

You may find yourself in situations in which He asks you to say or do something that seems ludicrous! But if you listen to His voice and trust Him, you'll find out that He's right every time. You may have to take risks sometimes in order to obey Him and say a particular thing, but if the Holy Spirit is in it, then it's the right thing to say. Take it from me—the one who called a woman's prized gumbo trash!

Jesse's Brother Wayne's Cajun Stove Top Pot Roast

4–5 pounds good grade chuck roast
1 package any good Cajun seasoning mix
2 medium onions, chopped
1 tablespoon garlic, minced

Place ½ cup–⅔ cup of vegetable oil in a 5–8 quart pot. Stir in 2 medium diced onions until onions start to brown. Season and cut roast in 1½–inch cubes. Trim away excess fat, leaving just a bit for flavor. Add meat and stir until meat starts to brown evenly on edges. Add water and boil down, stirring occasionally. Again, allow meat to brown somewhat (approximately 2 minutes). Repeat process, then add 1 tablespoon of minced garlic. Continue to allow water to boil down, stirring occasionally and testing meat for tenderness. Meat should be fork tender! Cook on high heat and do not leave unattended.

Pot roast takes approximately 2 or more hours of vigilance to cook, but it's worth every minute. Your patience will be rewarded. (If a little gravy is needed, just add about 2 ounces of water after third boil down.

Take off heat and cool for 10 minutes. Serve with hot rice. *Voila*—it's done!

10

Praying for a Hot Dog

I was in an airport one time, just sitting there looking at people. Have you ever noticed how people act when they get mad? My goodness, people get mad—especially, for example, if they don't get what they pay for.

I saw this man at a hot dog machine getting mad because the hot dog wouldn't come out. Boy, that guy was mad. He'd put some money in the machine and was going *bam! bam! bam!* on the machine because nothing was coming out. He was actually hitting the machine!

People get mad when they don't get what they've paid for. They'll start punching hot dog machines. They'll talk to them too: "Give me my hot dog. Boo!" You know, they'll do or say all kinds of

stupid things to a machine. I'm sure you've seen that kind of thing before.

I figured I had to teach that man to sit on his problems. So I went up to him and said, "What's the matter, sir?"

He said a few choice words: "Blankety-blank machine! It won't give me my hot dog!"

"Well, did you pray for it instead of beating it up?" I asked him.

He looked at me like I was insane. "Pray for a hot dog machine?" he asked me.

"I'm going to pray for this machine to give you your hot dog," I told him.

Well, it was a way to get the Word of God to him. You can laugh about that, but the man needed Jesus. When you're cussing at a hot dog machine in the airport, you need God, believe me.

I felt so stupid, though, laying my hands on that machine. Just as I was doing it, the devil spoke up: *Suppose the weenie doesn't come out? Then what?*

You know how that would look? Now *I* was the one talking to a machine. I was standing there laying hands on a machine and talking to it! It looked like I was doing no better than what that man had done! He was punching and cussing at it, and I was laying hands on it and praying for it!

I did it anyway. I laid my hands on that machine and said, "Devil, turn loose of that weenie! Turn loose of that thing in Jesus' name."

As soon as I said that, the hot dog fell out—*bam!* It fell out right there at the bottom of the machine like it was supposed to. The guy was shocked, and so was his friend. That man had a hippie friend, some dude who was standing right there watching. And when the hippie saw that hot dog drop down, he said, "Say, brother, can you get me one?"

That dude wanted a free hot dog!

"Naw," I said, "you've got to pay for yours!"

But the hot dog came out! I used that hot dog machine as a pulpit to proclaim the good news of the gospel. You laugh about that, but if you pull all the humor out of it, what do you have? I got to witness about Jesus because a hot dog machine didn't work! Did Jesus ever do that? Of course He did! He didn't use a hot dog machine, but He used other things to prove that God's power really works.

Remember the fig tree that Jesus cursed in Matthew 21:18-22? That's an example of a time when, like the hot dog machine, nothing came out! Jesus

cursed a fig tree and told it not to bear fruit. What happened? The tree died. The fig tree died, and no more fruit came out of it.

God will use miracles to proclaim His power. Jesus did it, and He wants us to do it too. There are people out there who need help. They've got terrible problems, and God will use anything—even hot dog machines—to prove He's real.

On second thought, I realized I should have prayed for that man's hot dog to come out with chili and mustard on it. That really would have been a miracle!

ban, the Cajun pronunciation of the French **bien** meaning well, O.K., alright, etc. Usually used together with the English as an affirmative reply. *"O.K., **ban,** alright, I'll see you later."*

II

A Night With a Swaying Demon

I'll tell you another story, but don't tell any-body that I told you. It's really a true story, but it's kind of embarrassing.

When I first got ahold of the faith message, I thought, *Well, bless God, I can do this!* Now, of course, any believer can talk faith, but there has to be some meat behind it too. Let me tell you what I mean.

After listening to tapes on faith, I said to myself, *If I ever see any devil, I'll just cast him out! And that's the way it's going to be.*

Back then I didn't stay in hotels when I was preaching meetings. In those days I just stayed in people's homes. And this one particular couple had just offered to let me stay in their beautiful home which had a nice guest room set up for people to stay in. It was a nice-sized room, and it was all fixed up for guests.

This couple told me, "Reverend Duplantis, you stay here with us. We have a swimming pool, and if you'd like to use it during the day, we won't bother you. You just enjoy yourself." I thanked them and agreed to stay there.

Well, that night I went into the guest room and started getting ready for bed. Now, what I usually like to do before going to bed is read the Word of God. That way, I put some Scripture in my mind before I go to sleep and the devil can't put anything else in it. I fill my mind up first with the Word of God. Most folks do that with their stomachs, but it works with their minds too.

So after reading the Word for a while, I fell off to sleep. But I woke back up at about 3 o'clock in the morning. As soon as I woke up, I saw this big gray thing just sort of waving from side to side at me. The first thing I thought was, *It's a devil.* I especially thought that since I was in somebody else's house. I just knew it was a devil!

I looked at that gray devil moving around in the corner and said, "Get out of here, devil, in Jesus' name!" But instead of leaving, the devil just looked at me. *This ain't working,* I thought. So being the great

man of faith and power that I am, I decided to say it again. I said, "Get out of here, in Jesus' name."

At about that time I heard the Lord say, *Well, why don't you just get out of that bed and go get him?*

Yoo, hooo hooo, I thought, *I ain't going out there!* Now, don't tell me you wouldn't have done the same thing. How many times have you had your leg hanging off the bed and the devil says, *There's a monster under your bed!* What do you do? You jerk that leg back up onto the bed where it's safe. And then you ask your husband to put the light on so you can go to the bathroom.

So I began to rebuke that devil from the bed. And every once in a while, it would move. Whooooh, that made me mad. I spit and screamed—and when I say screamed, I don't mean a low scream. I hollered. I used the blood of Jesus; that didn't work. I used the name of Jesus; that didn't work. I tried faith; that didn't work. I even tried grace. I did anything and everything to get that devil out of my room. "Get out of here!" I shouted at one point. I even stood up on the bed and walked toward the end and kind of provoked it.

"Get out of here!" I yelled. At that time I was a baby Christian. I still had my diapers on.

What a devil that was! He was stubborn. I spit and screamed at that stinking thing until 5 o'clock in the morning, and it wouldn't move. After a long time, daylight began to come through the window, and the room became lighter. I could see things better, and what I saw really made me mad.

That "devil" was nothing more than an old raincoat hanging on a rack!

A raincoat had kept me up for two-and-a-half hours—rebuking, rebuking, rebuking. Isn't it fun being saved? The reason it moved every now and again was that the air conditioner would kick on and blow on it.

Boy, I got mad at God. I said, "God!" in a really demanding tone.

What's wrong? He asked.

"I've been rebuking this raincoat for two-and-a-half hours. You *could* have let me in on it."

And the Lord said, *Jesse, that's the funniest thing I ever saw, you rebuking that raincoat, boy. You rebuked a raincoat!*

Now, did God really say that? Yes! Do you think I'd lie to you? The Lord's got a sense of humor. But remember, God told me to go over and take hold of that raincoat in the first place. I could have listened to God

and gotten some sleep that night. But instead, I stood on that bed rebuking a raincoat for over two hours!

Growing up spiritually is a lot like growing up naturally. You don't start out being an adult Christian. You start out by being a baby Christian, and baby Christians make mistakes. It's okay to be a baby, as long as you don't stay a baby. God will bring you along like the loving Father He is, as you grow into the full stature of Christ.

God *will* grow you up spiritually. But sometimes He'll do it with a sense of humor!

Jesse's Mother Velma's Chicken Gumbo

- ⅓ cup cooking oil
- ⅓ cup flour
- 2 chickens cut and separated
- 2 smoked sausage links cut in ⅛" slices
- 1-inch slab luncheon meat cut in ½" cubes
- 2 packages of wieners (cut in ½" slices if desired)
- 1 large onion, chopped

Cover bottom of 5–8 quart pot with vegetable oil and add flour. Stir frequently on medium heat until dark brown. Fill pot halfway with water and add chicken, sausage links, luncheon meat and wieners. Boil 35 minutes and add more water, filling pot to ¾ full while boiling. Turn off heat. Sprinkle filé lightly on top. Stir to mix filé, and then cover for 10 minutes. Lift cover and skim off excess grease. Stir and serve with hot rice.

12

Apologizing to Beau Jacque

Cathy and I used to have a little French poodle for a pet. I hated that dog. I mean I *hated* that dog! Even though it was a male, Cathy would put bows in his hair and paint his toenails. He was a weird dog, you understand? I hated that dog, because he was a sissy. Cathy loved that dog, and my daughter, Jodi, loved that dog, but I couldn't stand him.

The dog's name was Beau Jacque, because he had classy blood. His father's name was Beau Wattley, so he was from a good bloodline. All that meant to me was that we had to spend a fortune for him. Even though he was a toy, miniature white poodle, he cost a lot of money. That only made me hate him more.

Beau Jacque was a heathen, too. He was a heathen dog! I mean, I caught him messing around with the neighbor's dog. And the neighbor would say, "Reverend, your dog's been messing around with my dog."

"He's not saved," I would explain. "I'm sorry. He's a hot little heathen."

I would have to call that dog over, and he'd just look at me. "You heathen!" I would yell at him. "You're going to hell! Messing around with all these dogs in the neighborhood...."

He would just look at me with guilt in his eyes. He'd be telling me, "I repent. I repent." But the temptation was greater than he could bear.

Cathy would wake me up first thing in the morning and say, "Go let Beau Jacque out." He had to go outside to do his business.

I hated letting that thing outside. I had to stand out there and *watch* him do his business, you understand. I'd say, "I don't want to go out there and watch that dog crunch up his back and all that kind of junk. I am an evangelist! I'm on television! People know me all over the country. And they're going to see me in the front yard with my dog's back all crunched up. That's embarrassing."

"Listen," she told me, "we have to take him out every morning. You take him out."

I hated that dog, and I told him so. I'd say, "I hate you, you understand. I can't stand your guts."

This dog was so spoiled that if you gave him a piece of meat, he wouldn't even chew it himself. No, you had to cut it up in little pieces for him so he could eat it. That's the truth. If I gave him a little chunk of meat (it didn't have to be big—the dog was flat-out lazy), he'd just hold it in his mouth. I'd say, "Eat it, fool!" He'd just look at me. I knew what he was saying. His eyes were telling me, "Cathy cuts it up smaller for me."

I hated that stinking dog! I wanted a big dog like a Great Dane, a Doberman pinscher or a pit bull. I wanted one that goes, *Houf, houf, houf,* you know—not one that goes, *Wrrrrrf, wrrrrrrf.*

I was out in the yard one time letting Beau Jacque do his business, looking around to make sure no one saw me, because if they saw me they would say, "How you doing, Reverend? Oh, yeah, I see what you're doing there. You're watching your dog do his business, huh?"

"Hurry up, Beau Jacque!" I would yell. "Get behind the monkey grass, you understand? Man!" I hated that dog. The Lord knew it, and the dog knew it!

One time I took Beau Jacque out to do his business, and this guy came by walking a huge pit bull. Little Beau Jacque saw that pit bull, and the pit bull saw Beau Jacque. They started to get territorial. The pit bull stopped and put a paw on Beau Jacque's grass. Oh, that sent Beau Jacque standing straight up. That made him mad. Beau Jacque went, *Hrrrrrrrrr.*

I said, "Woaaaaaa."

Hrrrrrrrrr, he cried.

"Get down with your bad self, Beau Jacque!" I said. "Oh, you've got some Duplantis blood in you, do ya? Then go over there and take care of that big boy. Bust him!"

Man, that pit bull got all four paws on Beau Jacque's grass, and when he did, Beau Jacque went, *Hrrrrrrrrr,* and took off. Beau Jacque ran over and bit that dog's toe.

That dog was a great, big pit bull, and little Beau Jacque just bit him. Then Beau Jacque started trying to chew on his throat! You could see that pit bull just standing there with this tiny poodle trying to attach itself to its throat.

But the big dog didn't do anything to Beau Jacque, except go *Hrrrrrph!* And with that, Beau Jacque fell on

his back, going, *Hahhhhhhhh, ahhhhhhhh, ahghhhhhh, aghhhhhhhh.*

The man walking the pit bull said, "I think your dog's having a heart attack."

I said, "Get up, Beau Jacque. Get up!" And I was thinking, *Attack! Attack the dog!*

Beau Jacque was still going, *Ahhhhhhhh.* I had to go pick Beau Jacque up, because he couldn't even walk. His little heart was pounding, and you could see fear in his eyes. He was telling me, "Oh, thank you. That big dog almost killed me, man." It was embarrassing!

I had to take Beau Jacque in to Cathy, who took one look at him and grabbed him up, saying, "Mamma loves you, Beau Jacque." She was kissing him, and you could just see Beau Jacque panting and saying, "I almost died. Almost died."

Beau Jacque recovered, but I still hated him. So one day the Lord said to me, *I want you to call that dog over to you.*

"What?"

He said, *That dog knows you have animosity toward him. He's one of my creations, and I want you to call him over.*

"I don't like that dog," I said.

I don't care, God said. *I sent him to you. Your wife and your daughter love that dog. He's part of your family.*

Now you call that dog here. God spoke this to me, whether you believe it or not.

He told me to apologize to that dog.

I said, "God, I ain't going to apologize to no dog."

You apologize to that dog, He insisted.

Well, I felt so stupid. But I called him over and said, "Beau Jacque, come here." He jumped up and looked at me with these crying eyes. I said, "Listen...." And I could see it in his eyes. He was saying, "Go ahead, humble yourself." He knew what I had to do, and he wasn't going to make it easy for me.

"Beau Jacque," I continued, "you know I hate your guts, but the Lord said for me to do this." Now, whether you believe it or not, this is the truth. God made me do this, because I was wrong to that dog. I was wrong to one of His creations. I had hated that dog.

"Beau Jacque, the Lord told me to apologize." And I could see these tears start coming out of his little eyes.

He made a face like, "I forgive you. I've always loved you, but you never loved me." And so he tried to lick me.

"Don't you put your tongue on me!" I yelled. "I don't want your tongue on me. Heel! Beau Jacque, heel!"

"But, look," I said, "I'm sorry. I've shown you great animosity. You know I just want you to be a big dog. I want you to be mean and tough, you understand?

He understood everything I said. I know he did. That dog had a brain.

So I promised not to be so cruel to him anymore. I promised him I would never wake him up again in the middle of the night and show him a newspaper.

See, if God can't get your attention with higher life forms, He will use lower forms to get your attention. He will make you see where you are from His perspective. We're all part of God's creation. God created every living creature, and He expects us to respect them.

I had to humble myself and start respecting God's creation. My wife and daughter loved Beau Jacque, and I wasn't respecting that. But God got my attention, and I changed. God taught me a lesson through that dog.

bye, **bayou**
*"Get out dat pirogue,
you gonna drown in dat **bye!**"*

13

"i LiKE VariCOSE VEiNS!"

Now, I want you to know that I don't ordinarily look at other women. I'm not the kind of guy who notices them. In fact, I don't notice much of anything around me unless it's really in my face. For me to notice something, it's really got to be right up in my face. I don't notice half the things that go on around me. Let me tell you what I'm talking about.

There was a woman at a department store Cathy and I went to one time, and she was just beautiful. She had just finished cutting a commercial for the store, and she was looking great. There were men standing around with their mouths hanging open and every-thing. You could hear their wives saying to them, "Close your mouth, honey."

Now, if Cathy thinks I might be looking at another woman, she always says the same thing: "Are

you enjoying the scenery?" Well, Cathy saw this beautiful woman, but I didn't see her. The woman was tall with long legs and a short dress. She was a gorgeous woman.

Cathy said, "Just look at that girl."

I wasn't even trying to look at a beautiful girl; I was looking for a Chinese vase. I get my mind on something, boy, and that's what I'm focused on. I wanted to go get that vase—I didn't want to look at a beautiful girl.

But Cathy told me to look at this beautiful girl, so I said, "Where?" Then I saw this lady, and I saw all the men going, "Hoooooo hoooo."

All the women were going, "Pffft, pffft, pfff." You know how women are. They're like cats—their fur comes up a little bit, bless them. You can tell when they get territorial. They just go along looking distracted, saying, "Hmm, humm, humm." But you've got to watch them. You can hear them muttering, "hmmm, hummm," and all of a sudden, *whack!* They'll just slap a man in a second for looking at some other woman.

Anyway, I looked at that beautiful woman and said, "Boy, look at her. Cathy, she's the kind of woman men lo-ove."

Cathy looked a little distracted as I said that. She started going, "Hmmm, hmmm." That's when I knew I had to be careful. She was acting like a cat beginning to flex its muscles before the strike.

"Cathy," I said, "men go crazy over women like her. Men love that kind of woman, Cathy."

Boy, by that time I knew Cathy was getting stirred up. I could see it coming. So I said, "Cathy, you don't have to worry about that sort of thing with your husband here. I don't like that kind of woman at all."

She kind of smiled.

I continued, "I like short women, with fat, stubby legs and veins hanging out. I like those varicose veins; that's what I like."

"So why do you like varicose veins?" Cathy asked me.

"Well," I said, "if you're driving your car and you lose your map, all you've got to do is just read your wife's legs. Just follow those veins. Turn right. Okay. Now left."

I looked at Cathy, and she was saying, "Yeah, yeah, yeah," and laughing.

I got myself out of trouble that way. I had to play down the beauty of that woman, and I used humor to do it. I wasn't telling my wife she had ugly

legs or anything like that. I was just making fun of
that situation. Sometimes humor is the best way to get
you out of a bad situation. Humor can be your friend.

I made a joke out of that situation, but I still
had to make my wife feel loved. Women need to be
honored by their husbands. The Bible tells husbands
to love their wives. That means husbands need to
make their wives feel special.

Husbands, you need to make your wife feel
like she's the most important girl in the room, even
if there's a TV model in there with you. You've got to
let her know that she's beautiful. That's called loving
your wife, and she'll thank you for it. You'll see, I
promise you!

Jesse's Wife Cathy's Coconut Delight Cake

1 box white cake mix
1 can condensed milk
1 can cream of coconut
1 medium container whipped topping
1 small bag shredded coconut

In a 9x13 cake pan, bake the white cake according to directions on the box. While the cake is cooling, pour the condensed milk and cream of coconut in a bowl and blend together with a fork. Pierce cake with a fork and slowly pour the cream mixture over the cooled cake, making sure that you saturate every part of it. Spread the whipped topping over the cake and sprinkle with coconut flakes. Refrigerate for at least one hour before serving.

14

A WORD OF REST

Have you ever had somebody come up to you and say, "Uh, excuse me, but the Lord gave me a word for you"? How many of you have ever had that happen to you? The first thing your mind does when you hear that is to look at the person giving the word and see if they look right or not. Because if they look like they could have a good word from God for you, you might listen. You're judging whether or not what this person has to say is really from God.

That happened to me one time. I had a young preacher come up to me and say, "Brother Jesse, I..." but he couldn't even finish his sentence because he was blubbering and crying so much. I thought, *What's the matter with this kid?*

"Brother Jesse," he said, "just let me minister to you. You have helped me so much in my life, I just want to minister back to you. You're such a blessing."

"Well, thank you," I said.

"I'll tell you one thing," he blubbered. "I want to be just like you."

"Now, stop," I said. "You don't want to be like me, because I make mistakes. You want to be like Christ. He doesn't make any mistakes."

"You're right, Brother Jesse," he said. "I want to be just like Jesus, but I want to minister to you. I don't know if this is the voice of God or not, but I believe God gave me a word for you."

Okay, son, I thought, *Give me what you've got.* I was ready to do what I always do when someone says he has a word for me. You probably do the same thing yourself. If it is good, I put it on the shelf. And if it works out to be right on, then fine. But if it turns out to be right off, then I let it fall off the shelf.

"Okay, give me what you've got, and let me see if it bears witness with my spirit," I told him.

So this kid said, "I believe God's telling me this, but I don't know, Brother Jesse. You judge it."

I certainly will, I was thinking to myself. I didn't tell him that, but that's exactly what I was thinking. "Well, okay, play it, son. Give me what you've got. What has the Lord told you for me?"

He was so nervous. "I just…you know…I'm young, and I just want you to listen to it."

"Okay, get on with it, son."

"Oh, the Lord told me to tell you that the devil can't stand before you. You run right over him. You kick his head off. Why, you just run at him with everything you've got. You beat his brains out!"

This kid's right on! I thought. *C'mon, boy. This is bearing witness.*

"The devil," he continued, "doesn't run over you; you just run over him. You bust him in the head. He sticks his ugly head up, and you just nail him, binding him and walking all over him. You just keep on doing the things God told you to do. Does that bear witness with you?" he asked me.

"Son," I said, "that's revelation knowledge. You are *right on!*"

"Okay," he said, "but I'll tell you what else God told me. God told me that the devil quit trying to get in front of you."

"Yeah, tell it, kid!" I said.

"The devil has started getting behind you."

"I know it, son. Now you're preaching."

"Now the devil is pushing you from behind," he continued. "He's saying, 'Come on, minister, preach! Feed the sheep!'"

Kid, I thought, *you just slipped out of the Spirit. You better get back in the flow, man. What happened?*

He continued, "The devil is telling you, 'Don't sleep! Why should you sleep? You're a faith man. You don't need to sleep. There are people dying and going to hell, and you're trying to rest your body! What's wrong with you? Get up! Go preach this gospel. There are people dying and going to hell right now. Get out there! There's no time to rest. Preach this gospel. Heal the sick. Raise the dead. Cast out devils!'"

Then he stopped speaking over me. I was speechless, but the kid still had more to say.

"You see, Brother Jesse," this young man told me, "if the devil can't defeat you from the front, he'll go behind you. He'll start pushing you. Is that right?"

"Uhhhhh. Whewww," I finally said. This kid was right on the button. I had averaged maybe two hours of sleep a night for two and a half years. I hadn't taken a Sunday off since 1978. Sometimes I preached five times on Sunday alone. Cathy usually had to drag me to bed. I was abusing my body, and the Lord knew it. I was headed for a burn-out.

Not anymore. After I heard that, I decided to take a rest. God was telling me that I wouldn't complete my ministry unless I learned how to rest my body.

Did you know that it is considered spiritual to rest? You have got to do it. God did it. The Bible says that after He finished working, God took out one day just to rest. That's our pattern for living. We're supposed to rest regularly.

The morning after I heard that word from that young preacher, my body was thanking me—I let myself sleep in!

byok, an offensive or overbearing person.
"Dats all a bunch of byoks at de license bureau."

15

Pajama jogging

I have a pair of pajamas that Cathy has faithfully tried to throw away for twenty years. They're so old they don't even have any elastic around the waist. It all wore off, so I have to either hold them up when I walk or tie a knot at the waist, or else they fall down on me. You know your pajamas are comfortable when they don't bind up around your waist *at all.* How many of you have a pair of pajamas like that?

But those aren't my good pajamas. I have some good pajamas that are new, and they stay up around the waist. They have pinstripes on them, and they look wonderful. It's a good thing that they look so good, too, because I needed to look sharp one night when I was wearing them.

I put on those pin-striped pajamas one night because I wanted to practice faith. You see, I had to prove that I was feeling good. The devil was trying to attack me with fear, telling me I was going to die. He was trying to tell me I was having a heart attack, but I checked my heartbeat. It was still there. So I just began to rebuke the devil. And do you know what else I did? I went for a jog.

This was 3 o'clock in the morning. I said, "I'll show you, devil!" I had on those good pin-striped pajamas, and I went outside and ran a mile. In my pajamas!

Well, I forgot that the police were out there at 3 o'clock in the morning too. They were wondering about me when they saw me running down the street at night in my pin-striped pajamas. They came up to me and said, "How are you doing, Reverend? Boy, we've never seen jogging shorts like those before."

"These are my new pajamas," I said. But I was thinking, *Oh, what am I doing out here? I shouldn't be out here in my pajamas.*

The policeman just said, "We won't tell nobody, Reverend."

"Don't worry about it," I said. "I'll tell the whole world about it next week," and I ran off into the night in my good pajamas.

It was a good thing I had God's favor with me that night! My circumstances turned around, and that which the devil had meant to use against me turned out to be a testimony for God. The devil tried to tell me I was having a heart attack, but I wasn't. The devil tried to get me in trouble with those policemen, but he couldn't.

Now, for Christians, that should always be the case. God can turn around a situation the devil meant to harm us. The Bible says that God will take that which was a curse and turn it into a blessing for us because He loves us. (Deut. 23:5.) God will do that for us every time. All we need to do is ask.

Jesse's Mother-in-Law Irene's Crab-Stuffed Potatoes

4 medium Idaho white potatoes
8 ounces of crab meat
½ cup butter
½ cup light cream
salt and pepper to taste
4 teaspoons grated onion
1 cup grated sharp cheddar cheese

Scrub potatoes well and dry thoroughly. Preheat oven to 325° and bake until you can pierce with a fork. Baking time is approximately 1 hour and 15 minutes. Then cut the potatoes lengthwise and scoop out the centers, being careful not to tear the skins. Set aside empty skins. Mash potatoes and whip with butter, cream, salt, onion and cheese. With a fork, mix crab meat into potato mixture. Refill potato skins with mixture. Sprinkle with paprika, and reheat in a 400° oven for 12–15 minutes.

16

The Night With the Church Rats

When I first got out into the ministry, I faced some pretty hard times. But I was just happy to be serving Jesus. I was so glad to be in the ministry that it really didn't matter how rough it got. Let me tell you, it did get rough, but I was still able to enjoy myself.

I used to go around preaching in different cities, and I would have to sleep in some pretty strange places. Sometimes I would stay at someone's home or in a church or in whatever else was available at the time. Some of these places were real rat holes, but I just enjoyed doing the work of the ministry—even when the rat holes had real live rats living in them!

I'll never forget this one place I had to sleep, man. This was a true rat hole, and I got the opportunity to meet one of the rats that lived in that hole! I was trying to get to sleep one night when I saw him.

He was watching me, waiting for me to fall off to sleep. I'd close one eye to see if he was checking me out, and he'd look at me. So I rebuked him in Jesus' name, and he ran off for a minute or two.

But pretty soon I'd be trying to fall asleep again, and he'd run back in. I was lying in bed, trying to sleep, and that rat came over, climbed up and sat right on top of my belly! There I was, trying to sleep, with a big rat sitting on top of my belly!

"God," I said, "I have a rat on my belly, and it's looking at me."

I figured God would have to get me out of this situation since it was His work I was doing in the first place. God told me to do something really spiritual about that rat. I heard the Lord say, *Spit at him.*

I couldn't spit at that rat! I was so frozen with fear with him sitting there on my belly that I had no spit. I mean, how would you feel if you had a rat on your belly while you're trying to sleep? I didn't know what to do. The rat was just sitting there looking at me. I knew I was bigger than the rat, but I was scared spitless. Finally I saved up enough saliva to spit at him, and I yelled, "I rebuke you!"

All that did was make the rat stand up on his back legs! So now I have no spit left in my mouth, and a giant rat is standing on his back legs on top of my belly. I didn't know what else to do. Maybe I should have laid hands on him, and he might have fallen out in the Holy Ghost! (I probably would have done that, too, but there was nobody there to catch him. I didn't want him to fall and hurt himself, you know.)

So I got mad at that rat. "I bind you!" I yelled at him.

That did it! He took off and ran all the way down my leg. I jumped up and started praising God— "Whew, Jesus! Whew! Whew!" Then I turned the light on and saw three of his little cousins in the corner. I took one look at those other rats and could tell what they were thinking. They were thinking, *This is a Cajun chicken we got here! I bet this boy tastes good!*

I spent the rest of the night praying in tongues. I didn't get a wink of sleep. The next morning I got out of there and told somebody about it.

"Yeah," he said, "those are church rats."

"I know," I said. "I can tell they are, because of the way they're prospering. They're the fattest rats I've ever seen in my life!"

I'll never forget the night that rat sat on my belly, just looking at me. What a night! The devil was trying to run me off, but I wouldn't go.

You see, I was happy to do those things for Jesus. I didn't complain either, because I was just happy to be in the ministry serving the Lord. I knew that if you persevere, the Lord will bless you. He will take care of you for being faithful and doing your part.

Now my part was to go into all the world and preach, so that's what I did. And I did it with a cheerful attitude. I figured that if Jesus could sleep in a manger, I could sleep in a rat hole.

JESSE'S MOTHER-IN-LAW IRENE'S OYSTER GUMBO

1 gallon oysters
1 gallon oyster water
2 cups oil
2 cups flour
4 large onions, chopped
2 cups green onions, chopped
1 cup parsley, chopped
4 tablespoons filé

Brown flour in oil until it turns dark brown, making a roux. Add onions and cook until they turn dark brown, being careful not to scorch or burn. Add oysters and oyster water. Bring to a boil. Add green onions, parsley and filé. Simmer for 45 minutes.

Serve over hot rice.

17

WaRNiNg, PLaNe PRoBLeMS!

It's fun being saved. But sometimes God will put you in funny situations *because* you are saved. For example, I was in Denver, Colorado, once waiting for a plane after preaching. I had just been to Montana, where I had preached at a college in Missoula. After that I flew to Salt Lake City, and from Salt Lake, I flew to Denver. Now I was headed to Dallas and then New Orleans.

I didn't want to go to all those places. I just wanted to go home to New Orleans. But where the Lord calls you to go, you've got to go. So I said, "Okay, Lord, I'll do it." I took the trip and was in Denver, where I was waiting for another plane to take me home. I hadn't been home in a while, and I couldn't wait to get there. I was just ready.

Well, I was standing in the Denver airport
waiting for them to start boarding, and I started praising God. I was standing there, and I said to myself,
*Boy, it's fun being saved. Father, I just thank You. Faith
cometh by hearing and hearing by the Word of God. I hear
Your Word. I read Your Word. I flow in Your anointing.*

Just then the Lord said, *Jesse, I don't want you to
get on that plane.*

I said, "What?"

There will be trouble on this plane, He said. *Don't
get on it.*

"Trouble?" I asked.

Don't get on the plane, He said again. *Take the
next flight.*

"Huh," I said. "But-but, Lord, I-I'd just kind of
like to go home, you know."

Don't get on the plane, He said, just as simply as that.

So I went over to the lady at the check-in counter
and asked, "When is the next flight to Dallas?"

"Nine hours from now," she said.

When I heard her say that, I told God I didn't
want to stay in the airport for nine hours.

God said, *You can preach for nine hours. There are
a lot of sinners here. You can let your light shine. Don't get
on this plane. There's damage to come.*

"Man, God," I said, "can't You just 'heal' it? At least until I get off the plane. You know, just fix it, huh?"

Don't, He said. *I'm telling you. Don't get on that plane.*

After I heard that, I had to adjust myself to staying in the airport, and I was about halfway ready when God said, *Now, I want you to go tell that ticket agent there are problems on this plane. Tell them not to load this plane and take off.*

"God," I said, "they're not going to listen! They're going to think I'm a fruitcake if I go up there and tell them that!"

I could see myself, saying, *Excuse me, but God told me for you all not to load this plane.* You know, that sounds kind of crazy. But when you know the voice of God, you've got to do what He says. I still fought it for a few minutes before I did anything.

It was getting close to the departure time, so I knew I had to do something. I decided to walk back up to the desk and tell the lady I would take the next flight. As I got up close to the desk, I saw a guy smoking a big cigar that he'd been chewing on. It was kind of gross the way he did it. This man was sitting close to the desk, so he could hear my conversation.

I walked up really close to where he was sitting and said, "Ma'am, ah, I'm going to take the next flight

out of here. Ah, I want to leave, but the Lord told me
there's going to be some damage to this plane. So you
might want to get another one. Don't fly this plane."

She looked at me and said, "Who told you?

"The Lord," I said.

"The Lord who?"

"The Lord, God—Jesus," I said.

And she went, "Oh. Heh, heh, heh." She didn't
believe what I was telling her.

"Lady, listen to what I'm saying," I said. "If
this plane takes off, we've got problems. I'm a man of
the Lord. I know you think I'm a fruitcake. I know it
sounds nuts, but don't fly this plane."

"Well," she said, "we're about ready to board."
She picked up the loudspeaker and called out the
boarding. People started getting up to get on the
plane, and the man with the cigar came over and
went, "Whooof!"

I felt so stupid.

God said, *You told them. That's all I asked you to do.*

Yeah, I told them, but they were looking at me
like I was crazy. Some of the people had heard me and
began to stare at me as they walked past. And that just
made me mad. They loaded the plane, and the devil

said, *Nine hours, my man. Nine hours. I'm going to drive you nuts for nine hours.*

The lady asked me, "Mister, are you getting on this plane?"

"Don't let that plane leave this gate," I told her. "I'm telling you, God said it. I want to go home more than anybody! I don't want to stay here nine hours. There's something wrong with this plane."

"There's nothing wrong with the plane, sir," she said. "Are you going to get on the plane, or are you going to stay here? Because if you stay, we're going to put you on standby. You may not make that flight nine hours from now either."

"No," I said, "I'm not getting on that plane."

"Fine," she said and closed the gate. *Boom!*

I was standing there, feeling like an idiot. I was outside the gate, and the devil started in on me: *Bozo brain. Fool. You idiot.*

I joined in with him: *Boy, you're right. Huh, yeah. You're an idiot, man.*

I sat there and watched as they pushed that plane to the runway. They fired up the engines— zzzzzZZZZZZ. I watched it, bless God. And they got all ready to taxi down the runway. Sure enough, the engines were running—you could hear them go, *srrrrrrRRRRRRR.* The pilot throttled it a little bit to start taxing like he was supposed to, and he went maybe twenty-five feet before the back end of the plane just blew up. The engine on the back of the plane just blew out black smoke. Something just went, *booo-dooom!*

"Oh-hooo! Ahhhhh, yeah!" I shouted. I couldn't help it. I said, "Ha, ha, ha, look there. It's not working!"

Smoke went all over the place, man, and people came flying down that emergency chute so fast. They were out of there! I was sitting there going, "Ha, ha, ha." I was just enjoying myself. The plane almost blew up, and I was celebrating.

Finally, they got all those people off the plane and headed back to the terminal. The people started coming back inside, and when that old boy with the cigar walked past, I just looked at him and smiled.

Within two hours, they had another plane ready to fly to Dallas. And just as they started boarding, that old guy with the cigar walked up and said, "Hey, Rev, is this one okay?"

"Yes, sir," I said. "It's okay."

"What seat you got?" he asked.

"I've got 10A."

He looked at the lady behind the desk and said, "I want 10B."

I had to smell that old cigar all the way to Dallas and on to New Orleans, but it was all right because the Lord was with us.

You know, God will honor you. He will honor you when you trust in Him. In fact, God honors you at the same time the devil makes you think you're the biggest idiot in town. I'm telling you, it's fun being saved! You know why it's fun being saved? Because he turns crazy situations like this one into something you can laugh about! And also because everywhere you go, God protects you.

God protects you when you go in and when you go out. (Ps. 121:8.) He's given His angels charge over you, and they will keep you safe in all your ways. (Psalm 91:11.) He's not worried about your safety, so why should you be? The Bible says a thousand may fall at your side, but it won't come near you. (Psalm 91:7.)

So the next time you get scared or think you're in trouble, just start praying those protection Scriptures over yourself. God turns situations around!

Jesse's Sister-in-Law Deborah's Crab Meat Dip

2 8-ounce packages cream cheese
6 tablespoons mayonnaise
2 teaspoons Dijon mustard
1 teaspoon sugar
½ teaspoon salt
1 pound lump crab meat

Combine all ingredients except crab until well blended. Stir in 1 pound lump crab meat. Put in chafing dish and keep hot while serving.

18

Tale of a Busted Water Pipe

The first house Cathy and I ever bought was a 910-square-foot job on blocks in Southern Louisiana. I honestly believe the Lord wanted me to buy this home to show me something. I remember when I walked through it for the first time—I put my hand on the doorknob, and about thirty-five roaches came out of nowhere. Roaches were all over my hand!

There must have been some dirty people living in that place before us. It was Roach City, USA. You could hear those roaches going, *Hey, food!* I had to spray that house every day for two weeks before we moved in—walls, floors and everything. There was no furniture in it, and before we put our furniture in, it was bare enough to see those dead roaches all over the place. They died, it seemed, by the millions. We got them all out though.

Now, in Southern Louisiana it doesn't get cold. It may freeze a little in the winter but not very often. So when the owner told me I might want to insulate the pipes before I bought that house, I kind of laughed.

"Insulate the pipes?" I asked. "I don't need to insulate pipes in Southern Louisiana!"

You have to understand—I am not a mechanical person. I don't fix things. Cathy is the fixer of all things in our family. If something's wrong with my Harley, for example, I send it to Cathy. Cathy can fix a Harley motorcycle. She likes getting into that stuff, and I like watching her. She does a good job.

Well, I never did insulate those pipes, and sure enough, a cold snap set in. They told us to run the water so the pipes wouldn't freeze, but we forgot to do it. You see, this was the first home we'd ever owned in our lives.

The morning after the freeze, we got up, turned on the water, and nothing came out. So I called my dad and told him what had happened. He said, "Your pipes froze, boy. But they may not have busted."

"Well, what is this sound?" I asked, "—this *whoooooooohhhhh* under my house?"

"They busted," he said.

"Ah, Dad, can you come help me?" I asked.

"No, I can't do it today, son," he told me.

"Dad," I said, "I've never fixed a busted pipe in my life. I don't know how to do that."

"Well, just heal up the crack," he explained. "Go get a joint of pipe, and find out what's busted. Cut the water off."

"Where at?" I asked.

"Usually it's in the front of your house by the street. It's called the main," he said. "Sometimes they've got valves. In that case, you don't have to go to the main valve. You may have a valve somewhere in your house, and you can cut that off and then fix it."

"Daddy," I said, "it's 30 degrees."

"Welcome to the world," he said.

"Daddy, I might have to crawl underneath the house. There's water and mud under there."

You'd be surprised at what else was under that house. But I had to go, so I put on my coveralls. I looked under there and saw a lake of water. I knew right then and there that I had to drag my body through that water and mud. And it was 30 degrees!

"Cathy!" I called. "You're the man of the house!" She answered, knowing what I was going to ask her.

I looked around and finally found a valve to turn off the water. Then I remembered what Dad had

said about a split pipe. So I looked it over, and sure enough, man, there was a split. The next thing I did was go to the store, where I bought the wrong-sized pipe. They sold me the wrong size, wouldn't you know it?

I got back under that house and unwittingly dragged myself through some broken glass, cutting myself in the process. And there were spiders everywhere saying, "Hi! Hello!" I needed help, so I called for backup.

"Cathy, Cathy!" I yelled.

"What?"

"I need some help."

"Oh, I can't come underneath that house," she told me. "There are spiders under there."

"There were forty-seven million roaches in it when we bought it," I yelled. "They just moved downstairs."

"I can't go under there," she said.

"Why not?"

"It's dirty."

"So?"

"I can't do that," she said. "But I will help you."

"All right," I said. I was trying to back this piece of pipe out, and I was getting mad. I was busting my knuckles. It was cold. Even my blood was hurting. I started using words nobody had ever heard before: "Kew! Kou! Jes! Dp tht! Nom!" I even reverted to my Catholic days, "Jesus, Mary, Joseph! Jesus, Mary, Joseph! God!"

I was a preacher, you know. But I was getting madder and madder because I couldn't get the pipe to work. I was testing out different ways to get it to work, but it wasn't happening. I saw two lines, but I couldn't figure out which was which. *Is this the cold line or the hot line?* I thought to myself. I looked for the difference between the two lines, but I had a hard time finding it.

"I ain't stupid," I said, talking out loud to myself. "Okay, that's where the hot water is. Okay, that's the cold." I was talking my way through it.

"Cathy! There's a...there's a knob—there are two knobs! One on the left, one on the right."

Now, I was hollering this through the floor. I was underneath that floor layer, and from under there I yelled, "Don't touch the left knob! That's the hot water."

"Okay."

"Turn on the right knob," I yelled.

"Why?"

"Well, because the cold line's fixed. I can cut it off, but the hot line's busted and open now."

"Okay."

So what does she do? She turns on the left knob!
Wheeeeesh! hot water comes pouring out. I was scalded!
"Ah! Da! Turn it off! TURN IT OFF!"

"What? WHAT?"

"TURN IT OFF! I am being burned!" I was so mad
that I had a fit of carnality. The Lord had to tell me,
Jesse! Control yourself.

I said, "You're not the one, Lord, lying on your
back in this mud with a crazy woman using hot water
to try to kill You!"

"Cathy! CATHY! *CATHY!*" I hollered.

Finally, she said, "Oh, I'm sorry, I turned the
wrong knob."

I was lying in hot water. I'm serious. It was
all over me, and I was burned. There were spiders
looking at me, and my back was cut.

I said, "Cathy! Come here."

She came out, and I saw her little head looking
under the house. "Jesse!" she said, "don't move."

I was thinking, *Oh no, there's a snake here.* "What's
the problem?"

"Don't move!"

I could hardly move anyway! And all the while I
was under there, I kept smelling something terrible.

She said, "Don't move. There's a dead cat by your head."

I leaned over, and sure enough, there was a cat with his brain hanging out right there. I went, "Ahhhhhhhh, man! Grab it!"

"I don't touch dead cats," she told me.

I had a fit, I was so mad.

"CATHY! Grab that cat!" I yelled.

"I am not touching it."

"Yes, you are!"

"I am not touching that cat."

So I started to grab that cat with a stick, and all of a sudden I went, "Ahhhhhhh!" Something had stuck me in the back.

"What is that!" I shouted as I pulled what felt like a thorn out of my back. "What is this?"

"Oh," she said, "I threw some cactus underneath the house."

Glass! Spiders! Scalding water! A dead cat with brains hanging out! And now a cactus! I had another fit of carnality.

"I don't care about this busted pipe anymore," I said. I looked at the cut glass, cactus, guts and every-thing else lying around me. I had a dead cat in one hand and in the other a wrench that I was about to hit

something with. I came flying out from under that house! All I can say is, thank God my next-door neighbor showed up just then.

"How are you doing, preacher?" he asked.

I went, "Huh?"

He looked at me and said, "You know, I wouldn't touch that dead cat if I were you. What's the problem?"

I had been witnessing to this man, and I didn't want him to see me like this.

He said, "Go ahead and cuss if you want to. I won't tell nobody."

Every time you have a fit of carnality, you can take it to the bank that there's going to be somebody who will see you do it. He looked at me and said, "Your wife won't help you, huh?"

"How'd you know that?" I asked.

"Well," he said, "I busted a pipe earlier this morning, and I tried to get my wife to help. She wouldn't help me either. You want me to give you a hand?"

"Yeah, both of them," I said.

Well, we finally got that thing fixed, but it took both of us to do it.

But it was amazing. I was about ready to lose it, and here was a man whom I had been witnessing to, a man whom I'd been telling, "Jesus is the greatest thing in the world. Give your problems to Jesus. He can handle anything."

Now, I was acting like Jesus could handle anything—except for a broken pipe, a dead cat and an uncooperative wife. That's what it looked like. My actions were witnessing to him more than my words. I was speaking to him by my fits of carnality—my yelling and screaming and raging.

Let me tell you something. People are going to watch what you do. They won't listen to what you say as much as they will watch what you do. You could be the greatest preacher in the world, but if you go home and yell at your wife and have fits of carnality, that's going to ruin your witness. Your actions are your witness too. That's why it's important to watch not only what you say, but watch what you do.

CHU CHUT, a general purpose substitute for naming any small object or device.
"De motor wont run wit dat little chu chut dere."

19

PRAYING LiKE MARY PRAYED

One day a lady stopped by my office while I was working. Now, usually I'm never in my office, but I happened to be there when this lady dropped by. When she came through the main doors, she saw me and said, "Oh, Brother Jesse!" to get my attention. I had never seen her before.

I said, "Hello, how are you doing?"

"Brother Jesse, I need to ask you a question," she said. "I need to ask you a question right now, because you have disturbed me."

I thought to myself, *Oh, God, what have I done now?*

"I have?" I asked.

"Yes," she said. "We watch your television program all the time."

"Well, thank you," I said. "That's very kind of you to do that. What can I do for you?"

"You don't like Mary, do you?" She asked me the question just like that.

"What?" I said. I didn't even know what she was talking about.

"You don't like Mary."

"Mary who?"

"The Virgin Mary," she said. "You don't like her, do you?"

"Yes, I do," I said. "What makes you think I don't like Mary?"

"Because I heard you say you don't pray to Mary." She said "I heard you say that in one of your sermons. You don't pray to Mary."

She continued, "I love Mary. I have several ladies who come to my house, and we pray every day to Mary. And we pray the rosary. We love Mary. But I want to let you know that we're also Spirit filled, and we love God. We just pray to Mary. Now you're telling me, you don't."

This lady was upset. I knew I could've hit her right between the chops with a theological, hermeneutical, philosophical slap. But I wanted to build a bridge instead of burn one. So I said nicely, "Why, I love Mary. The Bible says she's found favor among all women. She's the mother of Jesus."

"Well," she said, "why don't you like to pray to her?"

Now this was a very sincere woman who loved God. You could see that. That woman loved Jesus Christ. She was born again, and she loved God with all of her heart.

"You're right," I said. "I don't pray to Mary."

"You don't pray to Mary?" she asked.

"No, ma'am, I don't." I replied.

"Well, why not?"

"Because I pray like Mary prayed," I said.

"What?"

"You mean to tell me you don't pray like Mary prayed?" I asked that woman.

"Like Mary prayed?" she asked.

"You mean to tell me, as much as you love Mary, you don't pray like Mary prayed?"

She said, "Uh, well, no, not really. Ah, well, how did Mary pray?"

"Well," I said, "she prayed like her Son told her to pray. You mean to tell me all this time that you've loved Mary, you're not praying like Mary prayed? I'm shocked. *I am shocked!*"

"Well, how did Mary pray?" she asked.

"She prayed exactly like Jesus told her to pray—she prayed to the Father in Jesus' name," I said. "Don't you pray like that? Wouldn't you want to pray like Mary prayed?"

"Yes," she said, "I want to pray like Mary prayed."

"Well," I said, "this is how she prayed. 'Father, in the name of Jesus, I speak Your Word today.' Did you know Mary was in the Upper Room and filled with the Holy Spirit just like Philip, James and John?"

I asked that woman, "Don't you want to pray like Mary prayed? Girl, as much as you love Mary, you ought to at least pray like Mary prayed!"

"Huh, I see," she said. "I'm going to start praying like Mary prayed."

"You need to do that," I said. "When you pray, you ask the Father in Jesus' name, and the Bible says He will bless you."

Man, she left my office all smiles. She went to her little Bible study, and when they all started praying to Mary, she said, "No, no, no, we're not doing that any more."

They said, "Well, why not?"

"We're going to pray like Mary prayed," she announced. "We're going to pray like Mary prayed from now on."

"How did Mary pray?" they asked.

"Brother Jesse said Mary prayed like this." And she showed them how Jesus told Mary to pray.

Now all of them are praying like Mary prayed. They invited this priest over to their prayer meeting and said, "Don't you want to pray like Mary prayed?"

"Well," the priest said, "I don't know. How did Mary pray?"

She said, "Brother Jesse said, 'This is how Mary prayed.'" And she told him what I had told her.

Now the priest is praying like Mary prayed, I'm praying like Mary prayed and that whole Bible study group is praying like Mary prayed. Glory to God!

What did I do? I built a bridge. I could have hurt that lady, but I could see she loved God. I didn't get all dogmatic on her. Instead, I helped her, and now they're all filled with more of the Holy Ghost. Now they've got people coming to that prayer meeting who are getting blessed. They are ministering to the priest! They pray, give altar calls after mass and lay hands on the sick. They fall out in the Spirit and get healed.

It worked. Instead of hurting somebody and taking something very, very sacred and making a religious argument over it, I helped her. That's our job as Christians. We don't need to be dogmatic with

people who are sincere and love God. We can build
bridges; we can bring people closer together, not talk
about our differences.

JESSE'S "TaNTE" MEL'S CRaCKER PUDDiNG

    3 ¾ cups milk
    ¾   cup sugar
    4 ½ tablespoons flour
    3   eggs
    1   tablespoon vanilla
    1   box saltine crackers

Bring milk to a boil, and set to the side. In a
separate bowl, mix sugar and flour. Stir in eggs until
well mixed. Add milk to mixture a little at a time,
stirring constantly. Return mixture to heat and cook
on low, stirring constantly until thickened. Mixture
should coat spoon.

In a large bowl, layer pudding and crackers, ending
with pudding on top. Refrigerate until time to serve.

20

WOMAN OF SEVENTY-TWO NEEDS A MAN!

After a crusade one night in Shreveport, Louisiana, a few years ago, I ran into this old lady who attacked me. I had just finished preaching and was coming off the platform with two guards at my sides when I got attacked. I walked out with guards like that because in some cities people will knock you down, you know.

As I walked through the side entrance of the auditorium, I saw a seventy-two-year-old woman standing there. First of all, when you see a seventy-two-year-old woman, you don't ever say anything to her about violating security and being in restricted places. Now, you get a guy or even a young woman in a restricted area, and security will be all over that person. But a grandmother is no threat to anyone.

She was a sweet-looking little grandmother. She could get by security more often than anyone else you've ever seen. There she was. I saw her as I was walking by, and she was just smiling away at me.

So I said, "How are you doing?"

As soon as I said that, she grabbed me and threw me into a closet. She just pushed me in and then jumped in after me—right in front of these security guards! She slammed the door, looked at me and said, "I want a man!"

I said, "You've got to be kidding me!"

"I want a man, and I want him now!" she said again.

I wanted to say, *Woman, open that door!*

Boy, I could just see the headlines, "Evangelist in a Closet With a Seventy-Two-Year-Old Woman."

"What?" I said.

"I want a man!" she said. "I'm not dead!"

I told her I didn't want to talk about her problem. I had a problem of my own right then. This didn't look good.

She said, "I lost my husband several years ago, and I'm tired of being alone! I want a man! You're a man of God, and you know how to pray. Pray for me!"

What was I supposed to do? I mean, wouldn't you have prayed for that woman if she'd had *you* in the closet?

"Lord, give her a man!" I prayed. "Whatever she needs, give him to her—but make sure he's strong." This was a strong woman, bless God. She needed a strong man.

"Now open the door!" I shouted.

The guards tried to open the door, but she beat them to it. She opened it up and said, "Thank you. The two of us agreed! I'm going to get me a man."

And I thought, *I don't doubt you will, sweetheart.*

I leaped out of that closet, and one of the guards said, "Brother Jesse, we're sorry, but that woman just threw you in the closet."

"Don't you ever let old women get around me anymore!" I told them.

Maybe eleven months later I had to go back to Shreveport. I was preaching for a pastor there at his church. And as I was getting ready to go out and preach, I decided to go visit my tape table. I very seldom ever go to my tape table, but I just wanted to go back there before the service.

So I walked back there, and all of a sudden, here came that old lady who had hijacked me into the closet!

I looked at her and saw right away that she had a man on her arm. And he was a good-looking man!

She looked at me and said, "Remember me?"

"Ah, yes, ma'am," I said.

"It worked," she said. "Look!" She gestured to the man. They were married, happy and blessed.

I looked at him and said, "Sir, are you in shape?"

"Yeah," he said. "I'm a jogger. I run about fifteen, twenty miles a week, and I eat right."

"You need to do that with her, don't you?" I said.

"How'd you know that?" he asked.

"Look," I said, "the Lord works in mysterious ways."

She was seventy-two. He was about seventy-four, but he didn't look it. She really didn't look seventy-two either. She looked about fifty-five, really. She was in good shape and was actually quite a pretty lady.

I talked to her more after the service. "Boy," I said, "you kind of shook me up back there in the closet last year."

"Well," she said, "I read a Scripture that day and did what it said."

"Which one was that?" I asked.

"'The violent take it by force.'" (Matt. 11:12.)

That lady took the Scripture literally. She didn't care what it meant. She just knew it was meant for her. And it worked.

Most people think you have to get down on your knees and pray and fast for weeks for God to answer your prayers. But did you know that God hears you the minute you pray? It's true! He's listening to you at the moment you turn to Him. And it doesn't take much to get your prayers answered. You just need simple faith like that seventy-two-year-old woman. She got ahold of a promise from God and believed it. God will honor that. And God will honor your prayers too.

> **coo,** a very enthusiastic
> expression of amazement.
> *"Coo! Look at de size of dem shrimp!"*

21

Accident at the Roller Rink

When I was a teenager, I tried to take up roller-skating. I tried to be cool, you know. But it's hard to be cool when you've got all these little kids skating around you, saying, "C'mon, fat boy, you can make it." I'd get embarrassed. And there was this girl that I was dating, and she was just laughing and skating around, leaving me stumbling.

Cathy and I used to go to a skating rink when we were teenagers, but it wasn't one of those beautiful skating rinks they've got all over the place now. It was an old skating rink with trashy wooden floors. They had big old Masonite blade fans in the corner to keep things cool.

I wanted to be cool when I went skating, but I couldn't even stand up with skates on. So I put them on and stood there, hanging onto the rail. I was looking

good, you know, not doing anything. I just stood there
with a big fan blowing through my hair.

Cathy told me that I probably didn't know how
to skate.

"Naw," I admitted, "but I'll learn."

Then this guy with a whistle got up and started
blowing, *"Broop, broop. Brooop,* c'mon, move, *broop,
broop,* get your hand off the rail!"

So I took it off, and *wham!* I hit the ground.

The man with the whistle didn't care if anybody
hit the ground. There was a storm blowing inside that
rink—that big fan was pushing things all over the
place, and kids were screaming by. With all that going
on, it took me a long time to get back up and grab the
rail again.

Cathy came over and asked, "You want me to
help you?"

"No, I can do it; I can do it," I said.

"There's just one thing I can't figure out," I
confessed. "How do you stop?"

You see, they had told me to just put my foot
forward and that little rubber thing would stop me.
Well, I tried that. I put *both* of those rubber stops down
at the same time and *waddup, waddup, wham!* my body
hit those old wooden floors twice as hard.

But I was still trying to get it. The storm was blowing from that big fan, boy. *Whooooo.* Kids were going around me, laughing: "Ha, ha, ha. Ha, ha," and I started to fall with my arms waving all over the place. I caught one of those kids as I was falling, and I slapped him as I went down. *Whack!* I still enjoy thinking about that slap, and that's been over thirty years ago.

Well, finally, I got going. I started really going— except that I didn't know how to turn. Just then, some kid pushed me, and I started heading straight for the fan!

Like I said, it was a big old fan with Masonite blades and no screen. It was just blowing to keep the air moving. I ran right into it! I couldn't stop. I went "Ahhhhyhhhhhhhh!" and caught it by the blades. I had to wrestle with it to keep it from cutting me. I fought that fan, and it was going, *arhhh, arhhh, arhhhh.* Blue smoke came out, and the whistle guy showed up: *"Breep, breep, breeep.* Turn it loose!" he said. "Turn it loose!"

"No," I screamed, "that thing will eat my lunch if I turn it loose, Jack."

I burned up the fan motor! *Errrh, errrh, errrrrh,* it groaned. They had to shut down the skating rink for a while just to get me out of the fan. I wanted to get out of there, but I couldn't. My hands were all cut up.

After I broke the fan, everybody hollered at me, "You burned up the fan! You burned it up!" I should've thrown *them* into that fan.

Just then Cathy came over to me and grabbed my hand. She knew I didn't know how to skate, but she helped me. We just kept at it, taking those curves slow, and it wasn't long before I was skating. I just needed a little help, that's all.

Things will come up in your life that will make you look stupid because you don't know how to do them. It doesn't mean that you are stupid; it just means that you haven't done that thing before. That's okay. We all have to start out somewhere. The secret is to be humble and ask for help if you need to.

How do you think I got to the place where I am in the ministry now? Certainly not without help. I had to have people show me what to do sometimes. Sure, I prayed and trusted in God to help me, but God also sends people to come alongside and take your hand, just like Cathy did in that skating rink. God will keep sending someone like that until, eventually, you can get out on your own two feet and skate all by yourself.

By the way, I still had to hit the wall a few times to slow down before I went into those turns!

Jesse's Mother-in-Law Irene's Crawfish Bisque

2	sticks of butter
4	eggs
1½	cups flour
	cooking oil (see directions for amount)
2	large onions, finely chopped
2	stalks of celery, finely chopped
4	tablespoons of parsley, finely chopped
1	bunch of green onion tops, chopped
4	pounds cooked crawfish tails, peeled and ground
*75–100	cleaned crawfish heads
1	large loaf French bread or 4 cups crumbled cornbread
	(If you use French bread, wet it and squeeze out excess water before adding to crawfish mixture)
	crawfish gravy (see recipe below)
	salt and pepper to taste

Sauté vegetables in butter until tender. Let cool. In a large mixing bowl, mix ground crawfish tails, sautéed vegetables, bread, slightly beaten eggs, salt and pepper. Mix well. Stuff crawfish heads with

mixture. Roll stuffed heads in flour and set aside. In a large frying pan, heat 1½ inches of cooking oil to medium-high heat. Fry floured heads until golden brown—about 10 minutes. Drain. In a large baking dish, layer heads, stuffing side up. Pour crawfish gravy over the heads. Bake at 350° until gravy thickens. Serve over hot rice.

*If you cannot get the crawfish heads, you can make loaves out of the crawfish mixture. Follow the above directions, but instead of stuffing the heads, separate mixture and shape into 2 medium or 4 small loaves. Coat loaves generously with flour. Place on a lightly buttered cookie sheet and bake until browned in a 350° oven. Transfer loaves to a large baking dish. Pour crawfish gravy over loaves and bake until gravy thickens.

Crawfish Gravy

½ cup flour
½ cup cooking oil
1 large onion, chopped
½ bell pepper, chopped
2 stalks celery, chopped
2 tablespoons parsley, chopped
2 tablespoons green onion tops, chopped
2 tablespoons Creole seasoning mix
1 pound cooked crawfish tails
4 cups water

Brown flour and oil in heavy saucepan on stove until medium brown (this is a roux). Add chopped onions, peppers and celery. Cook until tender. Continue cooking until mixture starts to stick to the bottom of the pot. Make sure you do not let it burn. Add water, parsley, onion tops and seasonings. Bring to a boil. Reduce heat to medium and cook for 15 minutes. Add crawfish. Reduce heat to low and simmer for 45 minutes.

22

Slow-Cruisin' Granny

Have any of you ever had fits of carnality since you became a Christian? As I've already told you, I have! I'm not proud of it, but I've had my share of fits of carnality. Do you know what I'm talking about? Have you had one today? Have you ever gotten up, a little tired like I have, and heard your kids screaming and hollering as you're trying to get to the convention where you're going to preach? I mean, sometimes it seems as if it's one thing after another.

This actually happened to me. I was late getting to the airport one time when I had a preaching engagement. I knew I should've been praying, but I just didn't feel like it. I was late, and I told Cathy I wanted to drive.

I wanted to make sure I was going to get to the airport on time. My daughter, who was about six years

old at the time, was in the backseat, and my wife was in the front. And I was taking us down the road in a hurry.

Here I was on my way to preach at a spiritual meeting, but I was about ready to encounter a fit of carnality.

Have you ever noticed that every time you're in a hurry, there's some grandma on the road slowing things down? Or there's an old man in front of you who can't hear anything. You can blow a Mack truck horn right behind him. It may even blow his trunk open, but he'll just keep looking straight ahead because he can't hear a thing.

It seems like when you're in a hurry like that, everybody who's not in a hurry gets on the road. For example, as we were on our way to the airport, this grandma came flying out in front of us, going about sixty miles an hour. But no sooner did she get in front of us than she slowed down to thirty-five miles an hour! Have you ever been there? Do you know that old woman? Yeah, sure you do.

So I was trying to get around her, but she thought both lanes belonged to her. I went to the left; she went to the left. I went to the right; she went to the right. I started feeling Tabasco sauce coming up my legs. I was praying like this: "God, do something with this woman!"

But I didn't wait for God to answer that prayer.
Instead, I began to talk to that woman. "Woman," I said,
"if you can't drive the car, park it!" Then I realized she
couldn't hear any of this. She had a bun of hair on the
back of her head that was acting as a radio antenna.
She was listening to something, but it wasn't me! She
didn't know about me, because she was tuned out.

This woman was starting to drive me nuts.
Every time she looked at something off to the left, her
car would drift over to the left with her. The same
thing happened when something on the right caught
her eye.

I was starting to explode, and Cathy was just
looking at me like, *I'm not getting involved in this carnality.* Of course she didn't say that. She was just looking
at me and thinking it.

"I'm *trying* to get to a meeting!" I yelled.

If only this woman in front of me would have
gone to the right a half-inch more, I could've gotten
around her. I wanted to put my foot in the carburetor,
swerve to the left and roar past. I didn't care if I hit the
grass. I didn't care if I went into the median. I *had* to
pass that old woman.

So I waited for my chance. I was watching her
closely in order to pull out and pass her when, all of a

sudden, the muffler fell off her car! That thing just came tumbling down the highway at me, and she didn't even know it! Her muffler just fell off the car! I saw it coming right for me and tried to swerve, but I didn't make it. That old muffler came rolling up, and I drove right over it. Immediately, I heard, *blublubblublaa.*

That lady's muffler cut my tires! I was trying to go preach a meeting, and an old woman's muffler fell off the back of her car and cut my tires! Oh, I had a fit. I had a first-class fit of carnality.

I looked at that old woman, and she didn't even stop. She just kept going! She didn't even know she was driving a car with no muffler on it. "You old woman!" I yelled. "If I could catch you, I'd—"

"You'd tell her that Jesus loves her, huh, Dad?" I heard my daughter say from the back seat.

Cathy looked at me and raised her eyebrows. She was waiting for what was going to come next. Well, I just looked back at Cathy with a look that said, *Go away from me, holy one.*

I was left by the side of the road with two flat tires, and meanwhile, that woman was driving off somewhere without a muffler. I don't doubt that the same woman is driving along somewhere at thirty-five miles right now without that muffler.

Do you know what I did wrong? Let me tell you. At the very first sign of trouble, I should have prayed. I could have said, "Lord, I'm kind of in a hurry. Would You mind moving that little lady over to the side?" I should have let God take care of the problem. It was His meeting I was going to, after all. But at the time, it seemed like it was much easier for me to holler through the glass at that old woman.

The Bible says that to be carnally minded is death, but to be spiritually minded is life and peace. (Rom. 8:6.) See, I didn't hold fast to sound words. The whole time that my blood was boiling, deep down I could hear the Holy Ghost saying, *Watch it. Watch it, now. You're going over into the death side.* At any point I could've stopped and listened to the Holy Ghost and changed my words. God could have turned the situation around entirely for me. But instead I chose death—and ended up with high blood pressure and two slashed tires!

Every time you get into trouble like that, you can choose a word of life or a word of death. Let me tell you right now, it's better to choose a word of life! And it won't get you flat tires either.

d, always used in place
of "th", i.e. dem people,
de car, dose apples, etc.
*"All **dough dis** is your boat,
dat is my motor."*

23

WORDS OF DESTINY

My wife has always kept her words pure, even when I wasn't saved. Back when we first got married, we were both heathens, but within three years, Cathy was born again and the only Christian in our marriage. I was still a heathen, and she thought everything I did was a sin. She saw everything as heathenism—especially me.

And I made sure she saw plenty of it too. I wanted her to see me sinning, because I figured if I could show her enough of it, I could stop her from praying for me. I thought if I could just get her depressed, she'd stop praying for me.

I used to think to myself, *I know what I'll do. I'll get more drunk. I'll smoke more dope. I'll do more crystal until it's in her face all the time. I'll even do some cocaine! That's what I need to do to get her attention. Get me some cocaine. I can snort it from fifty yards through a hundred-dollar bill.*

Let her just try to talk to me about Jesus while I'm on drugs! I'll just sin more to depress her.

Isn't that horrible? But that's exactly what I did. I sinned until I couldn't sin any more. I was getting tired of sinning. My body was tired—it could handle only so much abuse. Finally I just got sick of it. I literally got sick of sin.

When I was sick was the only time when I would agree with my family's prayers of healing. All the other times, I would oppose their prayers. But when I was miserable and sick, I would agree with them. I could be throwing up my guts and, at the same time, agreeing with prayers of healing. I would have my head over the toilet—a place where it should never be—and Cathy would come in and say, "Heal him, Lord."

And I would say, "Heal me, Jesus. Heal me, please."

Every time this happened, I would lie and promise never to do it again. But my wife knew I was lying, and so did God. The Lord would tell me I was lying, because He knew I would do it again.

Even though my words were lying words, Cathy's words were a sacred trust. Her words were being recorded in heaven and on earth. Eventually

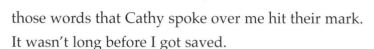

those words that Cathy spoke over me hit their mark. It wasn't long before I got saved.

Your destiny is in your words. God does for you what you say. God gives you what you allow Him to by the words you've spoken. You live your life by what you speak. It doesn't matter if you speak sound words, unsound words or no words at all—God is keeping track.

I realize that even the little, idle words I speak are being written down. God keeps the books. He doesn't forget. Sometimes I've wanted Him to forget. But the only time He forgets is when you ask for forgiveness and repentance. Then your idle words are washed away.

Words are a sacred trust to God. That's why He knew I was lying all those times when, as a heathen, I told him I would never sin again. I didn't mean it, and He knew it. Now that I am saved, I watch the kinds of words that I speak. I'll have to stand before those words I spoke in that great day. Why? Because words are a sacred trust between you and God.

Jesse's Mother-in-Law Irene's Crawfish Etouffee

2 pounds crawfish tails
½ cup cooking oil
½ cup flour
2 sticks butter
1 cup onion, chopped
1 cup bell pepper, chopped
½ cup celery, chopped
1 cup green onion tops
1 cup parsley, chopped
   salt, red and black pepper to taste

In a large saucepan, make a roux. Melt butter in a non-stick pot. Add to roux. Add onion, bell pepper and celery and cook on low heat until vegetables are wilted. Add crawfish tails and stir until all ingredients are completely mixed. Cover and cook on low heat for 10-15 minutes. Watch closely and stir often. The crawfish will produce water, and the sauce should be at the correct level. If the sauce is too thick, add small amounts of water to achieve the desired consistency. The gravy should be thick. Increase heat so that the mixture will begin to boil very slowly. Lower heat and add green onion tops and parsley. Cook for 6–8 minutes uncovered. Add salt and peppers to taste.
   Serve over hot rice. Serves 6–8.

24

THE INSANITY OF JESUS

I want to tell you about the insanity of Jesus.

You may ask, "What kind of statement is *that*, Brother Jesse?"

Well, what you've got to realize is that many non-Christians believe that Jesus was insane. It's true. Look at Jesus' mamma even. She thought He was *nuts*. His brothers thought that too. Even His own staff thought so.

Was Jesus insane? Well, they thought He was. They thought He was completely crazy.

Once, Jesus asked, "Who is My mother? Who are My brothers?"

Peter heard that and said, "My Lord, He doesn't even know His mamma anymore. Things are getting bad, Jack. There's no telling what's going to happen now." And His staff began to doubt Him.

Jesus was making people mad because He was healing the sick, raising the dead, casting out devils and breaking the bondage of religion. He was setting people free by the power that operated in His life. Why was that considered insanity? That was nothing more than the will of God. Yet people still thought Jesus was crazy.

Can't you just see His disciples huddled together? Peter's telling Matthew, "He's getting worse."

Jesus preached to the common people, but one day the Greeks came to see Him. We're talking about the Greeks here, you understand? We're talking Cadillac and Continental donkeys, Rolls Royce mules. They came to see the Man.

You could just see the disciples saying, "We're gonna eat out tonight, Jack, glory to God! Hallelujah! We're going to have us an offering tonight! We got the Greeks. Glory to God, the Greeks! These are not the Galilaeans. These are the Greeks!"

The Greeks walked up to Philip and Andrew and said, "We would see Jesus!" (John 12:21.) And the disciples thought, *Praise God! Wow! We got these boys on our side!*

The disciples said, "Well, just a minute; we'll go talk to Him." So Philip said, "Jesus? Jesus! Jesus, come here. Come on."

And Jesus said, "What, Philip?"

"Listen," Philip said, "You're going to love—you're gonna lo-ove this. There are some Greeks out there! The Greeks, Jesus! The intellectuals, the Ph.Ds. And they said, 'We would see Jesus.' Do You want to see them, Jesus?"

Jesus looked at him and said, "Hmmm. It's time for the Son of man to be glorified. If a corn of wheat falls on the ground and dies, it will abide by itself; but if it *dies,* it bringeth forth much fruit!" (John 12:24.)

Say, what? Philip must have been thinking, *Corn?* I can just imagine what went through Philip's mind. He's thinking, *Jesus is going nuts. Jesus said, "Ah, corn, wheat, die, abide." What's He talking about?*

So Philip went back to Andrew, and Andrew said, "Well, what'd He say? What'd He say? What'd He say?"

Philip tried to explain it to him. "He said—well, He said something about corn, wheat and dying. I don't know what He said!" Philip couldn't even repeat the thing, man. It was too confusing. Philip told Andrew, "It's one of those days. He's beside Himself again."

Andrew said, "Philip, you didn't explain it to Him right. These are the Greeks, man! The Greeks, you understand! The Greeks! Go over there and ask Him again."

So Philip goes back to Jesus and says, "Jesus, let me say this a little more slowly. The Greeks are outside. The Greeks, the Ph.Ds. You know, they could bless the ministry. We won't have to sleep on a hill tonight. We could sleep at the Marriott if You'd just talk to them. You understand? I don't mind sleeping on the grass, but a bed would be nice once in a while. And, Jesus, they said, 'We would see Jesus.' So, whatcha think?"

Jesus looks at Philip and says, **"Unless a grain of wheat falls into the earth and dies, it remains alone; but if it dies, it bears much fruit"** (John 12:24 RSV).

"Ehhh, ehhh, ehhh. Hehhhh. Ohhhhhhh," Philip says. "I see."

Philip had to go back to the Greeks and say, "Uh, fellas, yeah. He ain't seeing nobody today at all. He wants to fast and pray."

Jesus was insane according to the world, but He was in right fellowship according to God. Everyone else just had to get the right perspective on things in order to understand Him. Jesus was talking to a

bigger group than just the Greeks. His words were going out to the whole world! He was speaking truth that could set people free!

What did He mean when He said, "Unless a grain of wheat falls into the ground and dies, it remains alone; but if it dies, it produces much grain"? He was talking about His death, burial, resurrection and ascension. *Philip* was the one who was nuts! Philip couldn't figure out a thing because He thought *Jesus* was off His rocker.

And how many times has God told you to do something that made you think He was nuts? Maybe you decided you were going to give someone $20, but God said to give $100. You thought, *That's crazy! I can't give $100!* so you say, "But, God, that's a $100, and he doesn't even deserve it!" But God is simply trying to get you blessed. God sees the harvest your $100 will bring you.

God may tell you things that won't make sense right at the moment—things that even sound crazy at the time. But if God's really in it, it will make a whole lot of sense later. Remember, God can see the past, present and future. He knows what one little act of obedience can do for you or for someone else. He knows how much you will be blessed.

Sometimes it may seem crazy to believe what God tells you. But it's not—ultimately it's a blessing!

dubba, twofold
*"I got **dubba** my money back on dat deal."*

25

ANGELS IN THE CHOIR LOFT

Many years ago I was ministering in a small community church. It was a Tuesday night, and the sanctuary was packed. They were a pretty starchy group who were taught not to believe anything too "charismatic."

As the praise and worship ended, I got up to the pulpit, opened my Bible and began to share what the Lord had been stirring in my spirit. The anointing began to flow, and like I usually do, I got excited! Man, every point was flying out of my mouth like a speeding train! I was shouting and sweating—when suddenly the Words coming from my spirit just shook me to my shoes! I closed my eyes, clenched my fists tight and spun around, turning my back to the people and shouting, "Well, all right!" My fists were still clenched tight when I opened my eyes. What I saw made my jaw hit the floor.

There, sitting in the choir loft, was a host of angels! They were *huge!* They filled the choir loft, and shafts of white light literally beamed from their forms in every direction. And to top it off, each one was staring at me! I could hardly believe it—angels were kickin' back in the choir loft, just listening to the sermon! They were watching me preach!

For a minute or so, I stood with my back to the people in silence, staring into that choir loft in amazement. The congregation sat silent too, wondering what was going on and why I was looking at the back wall instead of preaching to them.

Finally I muttered, "Whoa!" When I did, a lady sitting in the back of the church jumped to her feet and screamed, "I see them too!" I turned back towards the congregation to see the lady staring with wide eyes and pointing her finger at the angels in the choir loft.

Suddenly, in one motion, the angels all stood to their feet and walked through the choir loft. The sight of it was so incredible and majestic that I could only stare in awe. As I watched these huge, gleaming angels walk towards the congregation, one of them turned towards me. He looked at me and then smiled. I watched him walk past, and then I looked into the face of the one behind him.

It was then that I began to notice what was happening in the congregation. The angels were walking through the people sitting in the pews. And as they did, whole pews full of people began falling out in the Spirit all at once! As the angels continued to walk, going straight through the sanctuary towards the back doors, I saw people bite the dust! Pew after pew, the angels continued to walk, until eventually they disappeared out the back doors of the church.

I looked at the congregation. Except for me, everyone in the building had fallen down under the power of the Spirit! Some had been knocked to the ground, others were sprawled out all over the pews and others had fallen sideways into the aisles. Even the sinners had fallen under the power. In fact, it looked like a bomb had hit the place!

With everybody knocked out, I didn't have anyone to talk to, so I just sat down. And from where I was sitting on the platform, I could see some people trying to get up and drag themselves down the aisles towards the back doors. They were trying to get out of the church! Later, someone told me that they'd found a man who had been in the foyer, crawling around on his knees and trying to find the door. He kept saying, "I'm not into this stuff—just let me out!"

The funny part is that the pastor of the church didn't believe in "falling out" in the Spirit. He pastored a church that taught against it! And there he and his wife were, laid out right on the front pew. They'd bit the dust along with the rest of their congregation!

Finally, people began to get up from the floor and the pews. And because hardly any of them had ever experienced the power of God in that way, they all began sharing what they had felt. Everyone testified to just about the same feeling. As one farmer put it, "I suddenly lost all my strength. I couldn't even stand up!"

It was a miracle and a breakthrough for that church concerning supernatural things. However, I found it interesting that only two people in the church actually saw the angels, yet all felt the power of them. God was trying to get something over to that church. He gave them two witnesses, but ultimately, He was trying to say, *Look people! I'm here in your midst whether you see Me or not!*

The Lord is in your midst everyday, whether you see Him or not. He is real. And His angels are His servants. There are things happening in the spirit realm that you may never see. You may not understand it all. And that's okay. You don't have to understand

everything God does. The important thing is that you recognize that He's God—that He's here night and day. He will never leave you nor forsake you. (Heb. 13:5.) You are not alone. And sometimes—if He wants to—He'll send angels to let you know just how close He is!

JESSE'S MOTHER-IN-LAW IRENE'S CRAWFISH-CORNBREAD DRESSING

½ cup butter

2 medium onions, chopped

2 small green peppers, chopped

2 celery sticks, chopped

4 cups crumbled cornbread

4 cups crawfish or shrimp, cooked and peeled

3 large hard boiled eggs, peeled and chopped

2 cans condensed cream of mushroom soup

3 tablespoons parsley, minced

1 teaspoon salt

1 teaspoon pepper

Preheat oven to 350° F.

In a large skillet, melt butter. Add onions, peppers and celery. Sauté for 5 minutes or until tender. Remove pan from heat. In a large mixing bowl, mix together cornbread, crawfish, eggs, soup, parsley, salt and pepper.

Spoon into greased 3-quart baking dish. If desired, dot top with additional butter. Bake for 25 minutes or until lightly browned. Serves 8.

26

"Prophesy Unto These Dead Bones!"

One time, I was invited to go preach at a church that I'd never visited before. I didn't even know the pastor, but a very well-respected preacher told me I should preach there. Now, usually I don't go to just any church, but I've always honored this well-respected preacher because he's such a fine man. He's a blessing sent from God, and since he suggested I go preach at this church, I went on his suggestion.

When he recommended it, though, I noticed he had a little smirk on his face. It was like he was laughing inside, *Heh, heh, heh.*

Well, I didn't ask him about that smirk. I just wondered why he said, "Jesse, you *need* to go preach at this church."

Later, when I was thinking about going to preach there, I called the pastor of that church. But like

a big fool, I called the pastor before I prayed about it. The pastor told me he wanted me to come, and I agreed. I told him when I would be there and hung up the phone.

I should've prayed more about that before I just agreed to go, but I didn't. I took the word of the power-packed, Holy Ghost-filled preacher who told me about it. What a mistake that turned out to be!

So when the time came, I flew to that city, and the pastor of that church picked me up at the airport. He introduced himself, and we got into the car and drove off. As we were driving, I started to tell him how glad I was that the Lord had allowed me to come and preach. After I said that, he turned and said something that blew my mind.

"I'll tell you what," he said. "I want you to beat these people. I *hate* these people. I *hate* the people in my church!"

I heard that, and it shocked my socks off. I was thinking to myself, *Goodbye. I'm out of here.*

He kept going, "I hate them, and they hate me. I hate every one of them! I want you to beat them up. *Beat* them, man. Do you understand?"

I'm not exaggerating. I was thinking, *Whoa, God. What did I get myself into?*

And he kept on going. He said again, "I hate them all!" He even cussed a little bit. He said, "And blankety-blank, I *hate 'em all!*"

I thought, *Oh, Jesus! What am I doing?* Then I thought of that preacher with the smirk who told me to come. *Ohhhhhh, God,* I thought, *what did he get me into? I* started going, "Bububu-bububbububu," praying in the Holy Ghost. I was praying, *Oh, Jesus, get me out of this. Translate me. Move me, God. Get me out. Get me out. Get me out of here!*

When we got to the church, I saw something else that shocked me. No sooner had we pulled into the parking lot than we saw two of that pastor's deacons having a fistfight. They were really going at it, *bam! bam!* punching each other! I thought, *Why does the pastor want me to beat up his people? They're doing a good enough job themselves.*

"Those are my two blankety-blank deacons," the pastor told me. "I hate those deacons." He started screaming, "I wish they'd leave my church!"

I couldn't believe what I was seeing. And that's not the half of it. I looked over at the front door of the church. Coming out was a woman trying to drag a pew out of the church! She was saying, "I paid for this pew. My name's on this pew, and I'm taking it home!" I

found out later that this woman lived in a mobile home. How was she going to put a pew inside a mobile home?

I was looking at all this, thinking, *God, we have made a mistake.*

God said, *Jesse, we did not make a mistake.*

I called Cathy and said, "Cathy, there are two guys fistfighting in the parking lot. And there's a woman dragging a pew out of the church."

That wasn't all! They also had to change the locks on the church because somebody was trying to get a piano out, claiming he had paid for it and wanted it back.

The pastor was cussing. He hated his congregation, and they hated him. I was saying, *Oh, gloom and despair and agony on me. Oh, deep, dark depression excessive misery–GOD!*

God said, *You're on your own, Jess.*

I prayed most of that night, "O, Lord, if it be Thy will—and I just know it has to be—I'll sneak out tonight. I'll leave the church door open so that man can get the piano if he wants to. I've got to get out of here, God! I can't stay here."

I'll never forget what happened that next morning. This church sat 1300 people—and it had only 45 people in it. The pastor stood up and announced he

had a guest speaker from New Orleans, Louisiana. He told them that another minister had told him that if he could get Jesse Duplantis to come to the church, then Jesse Duplantis could help them.

I heard that and thought, *Thanks a lot, guy. You're really helping me out here. Why don't you just shut up and give me the mike.*

I looked out across that congregation and didn't see how *any* help could come to *these* people!

As I stood up there, I noticed I had sweat running down the backs of my legs. I was getting really ticked at these people. I thought about starting out by saying, "You've been weighed in the balances and been found wanting. You're all going to *hell!* You're going to burn, you bunch of honkies!"

And I wanted to conclude by saying, "I'll see ya. Bye!" Out the door is where I wanted to go. I'd had enough. I was getting mad just being in the place. You see, when you get around people like that, they can rub off on you.

But instead of saying any of that, I stood up before those people, and I heard the Spirit of the Lord say, *Can these things be?*

I went, *What? You're asking me! Look at them. They're a bunch of heathens.*

God asked me, *Can these bones live?*

I said, *Only You know, God. It's not clear to me. These are a bunch of Draculas. This is the living dead here. They've been killing and eating each other, as far as I'm concerned. Oh, God!*

He said, *Prophesy unto these bones.* (This is how I got my message.)

I thought, *Prophesy? Prophesy what? I'm going to prophesy my getting out of here, that's what I'll prophecy. Bye-bye. I'm out of here. I'll say, "You understand, people, 'Thus saith Jesse, "Preacher get out of here."'" I'm gone. I'm out of here.*

I wanted to leave. I was finished, but God was just getting started.

He asked me again, *Can these bones live? Can these things be?* And when I opened my mouth, I began to spit and prophesy for forty-five minutes. I mean, I prophesied, bless God! And when it was over, I stopped.

I stopped and said, "Now, who wants to get saved?"

I heard someone shouting over and over, "I want to get saved! I want to get saved!" It was the pastor!

Then his wife stood up and said, "We have sinned a great sin. We're full of bitterness and malice."

Before I knew what was happening, both the pastor and his wife came to the front and knelt down.

And after they came up to the front, every single one of those forty-five people in the congregation stood up and followed. It was the first time in my life the whole church came forward and got saved! That much harvest came from the simple words, *Prophesy to these bones.*

That church today is running over a thousand members.

I'll never forget that story as long as I live. I got back and called my minister friend who had recommended me to that church, and I said, "Hey, buddy, this is Jesse."

When he heard it was me, he just laughed: "Ha, ha, ha, ha, ha, ha, ha, ha! Was that a hellhole, or what?" he asked me.

"Why did you ask me to go?" I asked.

"Jesse," he said, "I figured if anybody could bring revival to that place, you could. I didn't think there was any devil in hell who could wipe your smile off your face!"

"Well, it's gone right now," I told him.

I sure learned a lot from that experience. Those people were acting like spoiled little babies. They were having temper tantrums. They hadn't even gotten out of the diaper stage of Christianity.

I've seen babies right after they were born. Most babies are not very pretty right then. Their parents think so, but nobody else does. If asked about their babies, we all lie like dogs. We see a picture of a kid with his eyes swollen shut. It looks like he's been fighting with Mike Tyson or something. The baby's got blue bruises on its head where the forceps had to pull him out, and he's ugly. There's no other way to say it.

But the mother sees that baby and says, "Oh, look how pretty." The dad is standing there saying, "Uh, can we put this back? What is this?"

What am I trying to say? I'm saying that a baby needs help when it's young. You can't just neglect a baby like that pastor neglected his congregation. What good is it to have a baby if you're not going to parent it?

You're going to have to love baby Christians and show them lots of patience until they grow up a bit. That's what God was doing with that congregation. He was being long-suffering with them, and it paid off. They turned themselves around, and now they're growing in the ways of God.

gaga, someone prone to be too inquisitive,
(literally look, look)
*"Arrytime we pass in front of her house
dat gaga is rocking on de porch."*

27

CROSS-EYED HOLY GHOST PREACHER

You know how I got filled with the Holy Ghost? I got filled with the Holy Ghost by a cross-eyed preacher. He was as cross-eyed as a bat, son. This guy could be looking directly at you, and you couldn't tell it. This boy was cross-eyed!

He was not only cross-eyed, but he had a problem with the way he walked too. He walked like one of those old Pentecostal preachers, strutting around like a chicken scratching at the ground. I don't know why they all walked the same way. They didn't walk like normal people. Maybe that's kind of rude, but bless God, I thought, *What's the problem with this old boy?*

He talked like one of those old Pentecostal preachers too. He kept putting extra sounds at the end of his words. He would say, "I'll tell ya-ah-ah...I tell

ya, God-huuuhhhh, Gawd-huhhhhh." You know, I thought that the guy needed a healing for whatever he had that made him talk like that!

That's the kind of preacher who got me filled with the Holy Ghost. I was at that meeting with Cathy and her sister, Christine. At the end of the service, Cathy turned to me and said, "Go up there and get the Holy Ghost."

I said, "No way! I don't want to come back walking like that man! I ain't going up there!"

She said, "Well, my sister's going to go. You go with her."

"I don't *want* to go!" I said. "If I go up there and get what he's got, I'm going to start talking weird and walking funny."

"You need it!" Cathy insisted. "You've had an outpouring of supernatural power, but you need an outpouring of supernatural portion. You need the Holy Ghost."

I finally did go up there with her sister, but I put her in front of me. I said, "Go ahead, Christine. You go first."

As soon as I did that, an usher came over and grabbed me, moving me over beside her. So here I was, standing in front, and to be honest with you, I

was a little nervous. The preacher came walking over, and it was amazing what this man would do. He said, "I'll tell you, Gawwwwwd-huuuuuuh, Gawwwd-huuuuu, Gawd...."

When you see someone like this coming over to you, you've got to put your hands up before he stops in front of you. You want to blend in with everyone else, because if he stops in front of you, he's going to start scratching and shaking right there. Then everybody will start looking at you.

I could just see what was going to happen. I would be standing there with my hands up, and he would come over to me, start scratching and shaking, and I would start shaking too. Before you knew it, every one of us up there would be shaking and talking funny.

Well, he came over and stood right in front of me. I could see him standing right there in front of me, but he didn't know who was in front of him. I looked up and saw that crossed eye trying to catch me. It was moving, and I was moving back and forth, trying to catch it. He started saying, "Would you like to receive-uhhhhhhh?"

I was thinking, *Me? You mean me? Just who are you looking at?* I kept trying to move over to where that eye was looking. I couldn't tell who he was looking at. I really couldn't! One eye was looking at me, and the other one was on somebody else. He was standing right in front of me, but he was looking at two different people!

Christine nudged me and whispered, "Jesse, I think he's looking at you."

"No," I said, "his eye's on you."

"Yeah," she said, "but only one of them is. The other one's on you."

This cross-eyed preacher was standing in front of me, getting ready to lay hands on me, but he couldn't find me. He told me he was going to lay hands on me, and reached out his hand to touch my head. But his aim was way off. His hand was flapping air somewhere over between me and Christine, trying to catch one of us.

I realized he was seeing two heads, so I leaned over to catch that hand. I knew he was missing me because he couldn't find my head. And Christine thought he was going for her head, so we both tried to help him out, and *craaack!* Our heads knocked together.

She said, "I thought he was looking at me."

"No!" I said, "he was looking at me."

It didn't matter though. An outpouring of super-natural portion came upon me, and I was filled with the Holy Ghost. Christine was filled with the Holy Ghost too. Both of us walked away from that prayer line all cockeyed—but full of the Holy Ghost! It didn't matter what that preacher looked like. We still got the Holy Ghost.

God will use some of us who don't look the best. He didn't care that the man was cross-eyed. God just wanted a willing and obedient vessel. If you want to be used by God, determine to be a willing and obedient vessel. Then He can use you—no matter what your imperfections are!

Anyway, that's how I got filled with the Holy Ghost—from a cross-eyed vessel. Don't laugh. It could happen to you!

JESSE'S WIFE CATHY'S CREAMY SPICED SHRIMP PASTA

3 pounds fresh shrimp, peeled and cleaned
1 8-ounce carton sour cream
1 onion, sliced
¼ stick of butter
  Chef K Paul's seafood spices
1 8-ounce package angel hair pasta

In a large skillet, sauté shrimp, onion and spices in butter until thoroughly cooked. Add sour cream to mixture and stir until totally blended. Pour over angel hair pasta and serve.

28

Makeup—Don't Leave Home Without It!

I'm a Mary Kay cosmetics man myself. Glory to God, I've got this television makeup that I've got to wear. This stuff is something, but I have to wear it because I'm on television. But you can take it to the bank that if we go anywhere after the TV program, I'm taking it off before I go. I've been caught with it on out in public by accident, and I don't like that. People go, "Oh, hey, what exactly have you been doing?"

When I wear that makeup, the makeup people always tell me to pat my face rather than wiping at it if I get hot. I have to be real careful not to smear it. It's tough, and I'll tell you what—I could never be a woman. If I were a woman, I'd be the ugliest woman you ever saw. I don't see how ladies put this stuff on

everyday. But let me give ladies a prophesy, *Put it on!*
I tell my wife, "Don't leave home without it." I like it,
but not on me.

You know, it's amazing to me that a little
makeup can make that much of a difference. For
example, when you take your wife out to dinner,
she fixes herself up and looks really nice. She's got a
beautiful dress on, bless God. That makeup is perfect.
She's got those pouty lips, and you think, *Hey, Mamma!*
You look good.

You take her out to dinner at some nice place.
You know, it's the kind of place where they have those
menus you can't understand. And the waiters talk to
you in some foreign language.

And you say, "Yeah, whatever, brother."

They bring you stuff you haven't ever seen before.
The plates have all the different forks and spoons lined
up next to them. But you don't know what all that
stuff is for. (It helps to take a look around to see which
fork other people are using to know which fork you
should use. The only problem is that the other people
are waiting for *you* to pick up a fork first!)

Everything's really romantic. Your wife is sitting
across from you, and she smells so good. You can
smell her from across the table. She looks good too.

You want to hurry up with that dinner, she looks so good. You eat dinner in a hurry and tell her, "Honey, do we have to go anywhere else?"

"No," she says, let's go home."

Oh, vroom, vroom, vroom! *Let's go home.* Hallelujah!

You get home and open up the door for her. She walks in and says, "Lock the door. Lock the windows, turn off the telephone and hang up the Do Not Disturb sign." And she goes upstairs to the bedroom.

Just about then your kids come over, saying, "Hey, Daddy."

"Go home. Go home."

"But we need to talk to you," they say.

"Not now. Tomorrow. Bye."

"Where's Mamma?" they want to know.

"You don't want to know. Go!"

See, you've got power on your mind. You're thinking, *Yeah!*

"But Daddy…" comes the voice of one of your kids.

"Go home. Get out of here! Git!"

Finally, you run the kids off. You're thinking, *Boy, she had a beautiful dress on. She had on all that beautiful makeup, and she looked so gorgeous.* You're thinking, *Bless God, Jack!* You start strutting yourself. So you go into that bedroom—but she's not in there. She's coming

out of the bathroom, wearing this sack that you've been trying to throw away for at least fifty years, and all her makeup is off. She looks at you and says, "Hi."

"Turn off the light!" you say. "Just turn off the light. Why'd you take all that makeup off? What'd you do that for?"

"Well," she says, "I didn't want to smear it."

"We'll buy new sheets," you tell her. "We'll buy new pillows. Those things don't matter! Who cares?"

But women worry about these things. They pay attention to the little details, trying not to mess anything up. Men and women are different that way. But you don't want to magnify the differences; instead, you want to understand them. All the husband cares about is getting to the point. If a man loves his wife though, everything will be all right.

You see, the Bible says that we were created in God's image. (Gen. 1:26.) How many of you believe you were created by God? If you believe you were created by God, then you believe you were created in God's image. God said, **Let us make man in our image.** That tells us that God is not some gorilla hanging off a tree, eating a banana. That may sound simple, but some of the greatest intellectual minds of America believe it.

We look like God, and all of our ancestors did too! We were created in God's image and likeness. Now, we may have different personalities, but that's okay. God likes to have a little variety. That's why men and women are somewhat, but not altogether, different from each other. In God, it's all right to have different ways of expression, because God made us that way. That's the reason husbands and wives can match up so well— as long as they have godly love in their marriage.

God likes variety because He's a multi-faceted God. God made you in His likeness, but you have your own personality. Don't worry about covering up your apparent imperfections. Makeup may be nice on a face (hey, I like the stuff!), but you should never feel like you need to cover up the real you. You may be able to enhance what God gave you—and that's great. But just make sure to be who you are. Never lose the real you. God created you that way, and He likes it.

hayacall, used to denote any object or creature for which the name is unknown.
*"Dat **hayacall** jumped out de tree and ate him in de show."*

29

PREaCHiNg aT THE DiNER

"Do you boys love God?" my pastor would ask us, getting us pumped up to go out witnessing. I was only a young Christian at that time, and he was a radical fifty-nine-year-old pastor. He would look at a group of about five of us and ask, "You all got the fire to preach?"

"Yeah!" we would shout.

"So do I," he would say.

We would go to a diner sometimes, and no sooner would he get in that door than he'd start crying, "Oh, Jesus, they're all going to hell. Oh, Jesus! Oh, *God!*"

He would get out in the middle of the restaurant, lie on the floor and cry, "Jesus save them!" He would start yelling that, and that's all I needed to get started. When I saw that, I'd stand up in a booth, and I'd cry, *"Repent,* for the kingdom of God is at hand!"

That's all it took, boy. I would give that call and people would drop spoons and grits. Eggs would fly everywhere, but we'd continue to preach. We would preach up a storm, and then we'd get thrown out.

All five of us would do that. We had a great time. One of the boys who would come preaching with us was named Tommy. Now, Tommy loved God so much, but all he could say was, "That's the truth." That was all he ever said.

Pastor would be on the floor crying, I'd be shouting "Repent!" all over the place and Tommy would just back us up with, "That's the truth." Pretty soon Tommy would ask us to say something else so he could say his part again. And he would: "That's the truth."

One time we stopped at the post office, and Pastor said, "You all excuse me, boys. I've got to go in there and mail a letter." We were all in the van with him on our way to preach at a youth meeting. So Pastor went into the post office, and we waited in the van. We waited and waited, until finally we realized that he was not coming back out. So we shut off the engine and went inside to see what had happened.

We all went in there, and sure enough, as soon as we got inside, we saw him lying on the post office floor. He was crying, "God! Jesus, help these people."

God would touch his heart like that. He had a heart for souls.

He cried out to God for those people at the post office. The people in line must have been thinking, *What is going on?* When I walked in and saw Pastor on the floor, I joined right in. That's all I needed. I cried, *"Ohhhhhhhhhhhh!"*

Everyone suddenly stopped looking at Pastor and turned to see who this other guy was who was shouting like that. As soon as they saw me, I yelled, *"Repent,* for the kingdom of God is at hand! You're going to *hellllllllllllll!"*

You see, all I knew about was hell. I could only witness that far because God had just delivered me from hell. I didn't know anything else *but* hell. That was it. I'd say, "You're going to hell," and Tommy would say, "That's the truth."

People at that post office must have been saying, "I'm going to mail this letter some other time, Jack. I'm outta here."

We knew just enough about God to be dangerous, but we had made up our minds to use the information we had. We were determined not to know anything else but Jesus Christ and Him crucified. Everybody thought we were crazy, but that was all right. We got people saved just the same.

You don't have to be a deacon or an elder in a church to get people saved. All you need to have is the fire of God inside you trying to get out. Then just let it out. It'll get people saved!

Jesse's "Tante" Mel's Heavenly Hash Cake

- 4 eggs
- 2 cups sugar
- 1½ cups flour
- 2 sticks butter
- 1 pinch salt
- ⅓ cup cocoa
- ½ teaspoon vanilla
- ½ cup pecans
- 1 bag of large marshmallows
  icing (see recipe below)

Melt butter and cocoa together. Add eggs, sugar, flour, salt, vanilla and pecans. Bake at 350° for 35-45 minutes in a 10x13 inch baking pan.

Cut marshmallows in half while cake is baking and put on cake (sticky side down) as soon as you remove the cake from the oven.

Allow to cool before applying icing.

Icing

1   stick butter
⅓   cup cocoa
1   box powdered sugar
½   teaspoon vanilla
⅓   cup evaporated milk

Melt butter and cocoa together. Add powdered sugar, milk and vanilla. Mix well and pour over cooled cake.

30

PRaYiNg— NoT gaMBLiNg— oVER MY KiD

We all love babies, don't we? Babies are so wonderful when they're born. I'll never forget the day my own daughter was born. Jodi was born a Texan at Arlington Memorial Hospital. Everyone else in our family was born a Cajun in New Orleans, but my daughter is a Texan. We didn't know what to do about that. We wondered, *Should we buy her little cowboy boots? Should we dress her up in cowboy hats?* We didn't know how to dress her up.

Jodi was so beautiful when she was a baby. You should've seen her. Oh, God! It'd just take your heart away. I heard a nurse say, "This is a beautiful baby. She doesn't look like her father—she's beautiful."

"She looks like my wife," I said.

"Yes, she's perfect," the nurses agreed.

Yes, perfect. Jodi had perfect little lips and a perfect face—she was nothing like her daddy. You've got to understand how Brother Jesse looked in those days. I had long, chocolate-brown hair. I said things like, "Yah, man, that's mah kid."

I could see those nurses thinking, *Oh, my gosh, with a father like that, she could be smoking a joint at three months old. Oh, God, let's not let that beautiful baby go home with that rock musician! Why did her mommy marry him? Or is it a her? No, it's a him.*

I watched out for my little girl though. Once, when I didn't think they had fed her enough at the hospital, I had a fit. My daughter was behind the glass with all the other babies, and to me she looked hungry. I got so mad I almost broke the glass. I punched it, waking up all those babies, and shouting, "Hey! Feed my kid!" Some hunchback nurse came and got me.

I'll never forget that nurse. She walked all hunched over like she couldn't stand up straight. She said, "Come here. I don't think they feed them enough either. I'll make sure your baby's fed."

They fed my baby, and pretty soon we took her home. At home, I decided not to teach Jodi the traditions of Cajun people. I told her she was a Texan

and had to eat jalapenos. "Suck that burrito through the bottle," I joked. "Come on. You're a Texan. Your mamma and I are going to eat crayfish, but you have to eat burritos and tacos."

She began to grow up, and as she did, I would buy dresses for her. We would dress Jodi up in these pretty little dresses, and people would say, "Boy, you've got good taste." They didn't think I had taste because I looked like I was so full of the devil, but I knew pretty baby clothes when I saw them. They'd ask, "Is this your daughter?" when they saw us together.

"Isn't that a miracle?" I'd say.

"Yeah."

Time passes so quickly. It seemed like only yesterday that she was a baby. But then pretty soon she was getting married. My little baby girl was getting married, and I couldn't believe how quickly the time had gone by. I'll never forget when we walked down that aisle. I had her on my arm to give her away, and I was so proud of her. I walked her up to the platform, took the veil off and kissed her. I shook the groom's hand and said, "You're on your own now, Partner."

"Okay, Mr. Jesse," he said.

Then I walked up onto the platform to perform the ceremony, and the first thing I said was, "There's

no divorce in this family." I looked right at that boy who was standing next to my daughter.

"You hear me?" I asked him. "You love this woman?"

"Yes!" he said.

"Look at her," I said. "She's beautiful. Look at how beautiful she is."

"I think so too, Mr. Duplantis," he said.

"Take pictures now," I told him, "because one day she may come walking up to you without all the makeup and nice clothes."

Anyway, I said all that just to tell you how special Jodi is. But I knew she was going to be that way years before she walked down that aisle. Why? Because I wasn't at the casino trying to gamble on my child growing up to know Jesus. I knew I had a relationship with Jesus and He would do what He said. So I decided to take His Word at face value and pray for what I wanted—my child to serve the Lord and marry a man who would too.

I prayed that way for everything in my life. For example, every time I prayed over my body to be healed, it was healed. When I prayed over my wallet to receive finances, it got full. Everybody thought, *Who do you think you are?*

I'm not a gambler. You don't need to know how to hold 'em or know when to fold 'em. Not in God's Word. When you pray, you can *know* the answer's already been sent, bless God. You can pick up God's blessings by the barrell full, if you've got the guts to do it. Get out of that tradition, that stuff that makes the Word of God of no effect. It's not the gospel casino. It's the Word!

That's how I came to have a beautiful daughter just like I prayed for. It's called getting your prayers answered.

I, seldom pronounced as such.
In Cajun dialect: I is pronounced as ah,
but pronounced as e when preceeding a
consonant. Ex. in pronounced as een.

31

TaKiNg CaRe oF LuST

I'll never forget the time a preacher came up to me and said, "Brother Jesse, come here. I need to talk to you." I was thinking, *Oh no, he wants to counsel with me.* I very seldom counsel with people, because I'm not looking for counselors; I'm looking for comforters.

"Brother Jesse," he said, "come talk to me. I need to talk to you."

"About what?" I asked.

He took me by the arm and pulled me off to the side to some place private.

"Come here," he said.

"What?"

"Come here," he said.

"What, what?" I said.

"Come over here," he said again.

"Look, bud, I'm over here as much as I can get over. What do you want, I say?"

"Just listen to me," he said. "I've got to tell you something. I've got a problem. I've got a real problem!"

"Yeah, I can tell!" I said. "That's what it looks like, man. What's the problem?"

"I've got a problem," he said, "with lust in my heart. Lust, lust, lust. You know what I'm saying? I've got a problem with women, you see. What should I do?" he asked.

"Tell your wife!" I told him. "She'll stop it."

When a man tells his wife that he's got lust in his heart for other women, she'll put a stop to that right away! No wife will let that go on.

"Just tell your wife," I said. "Your wife is your best friend. All you've got to do is tell her, and she will say, 'Come here. I'll take care of that.'"

"Oh, I can't do that," he said.

"Okay," I said, "I will. Hey—!"

"No, no, no, brother," he said. "Wait, wait, wait!"

It was too late. That man's wife had already heard me and had started to come over to where we were standing.

"Come here," I said. "Come here. I want you to listen to this. Your husband is looking at other women.

He's got lust in his heart. What are you going to do about it?"

I just told her the way it was. I didn't mince any words or anything. I was honest about it, plain honest.

She heard that and said, "No problem. I can take care of that."

Now, why did I tell her that man's secret? I was trying to save his family. I was saving his children, and I was saving his life. Lust will tear up a marriage, but God is bigger than lust.

You don't have to have a problem with sin; sin should have a problem with you. The Bible says that the Greater One lives inside you. (1 John 4:4.) And if Jesus is on the inside of you, then He's greater than your problems.

Not too much later I asked that man how he was doing.

"Fine," he said. No doubt his wife took care of that man's lust problem.

Jesse's Mother Velma's Meatball Stew

- 3 pounds lean ground beef
- ½ box Italian bread crumbs
- 2 tablespoons garlic powder
- 1 medium onion, diced
- 3 medium-to-large potatoes, diced
  - salt and pepper to taste

In a large mixing bowl, combine ground beef, bread crumbs and garlic powder. Hand form meatballs to desired size and set aside.

Make a roux: cover bottom of a 5-quart pot with vegetable oil and add ⅔ cup of flour. Stir constantly until dark brown. Do not leave pot unattended. Add diced onion and sauté until fully cooked. Fill pot halfway with water. Bring to a boil and gently drop meatballs into boiling stew. Do not stir! Cook 10 minutes, and then stir, being careful not to break up the meatballs. Add seasoning to taste. Add diced potatoes. When potatoes are soft, the stew is done!

32

Getting into God, Not Religion

When I first started going to church as a boy, I couldn't find God there. I went to the place where He was supposed to be, and He wasn't there. In fact, church was the place where I learned to wind my watch. That's simply the truth. I didn't get anything out of church as a kid.

Before they were saved, my parents took our family to a Catholic church. Every Sunday we sat there for twenty-eight minutes. My Lord, if the priest hit thirty minutes, that was just too long.

Then Mom and Dad got saved and decided to go to a Baptist church. They went an hour! I would look over at my dad in church and say, "Dad, we've been in here an hour."

"Yeah," he would tell me, "I know."

"Well, let's go home," I would say. "An hour is two services in Catholic time. Do we have to come back here next week?"

"Yeah."

"The whole hour?" I would ask.

"Yeah."

"But, Daddy, it's an hour!" I would whine.

"Yeah, I know it's long, but that's the way it is."

Then Dad got filled with the Holy Ghost. After that, we never got out of church! We had to go to a Pentecostal church, and they didn't put a deadline on the length of their service.

There was one thing I could never understand about Pentecostal churches. How come they sing the same song over and over and over? They take a chorus and just beat it up. They sing that thing until you can't even remember what song it was. It's all just chorus—over and over and over. I would wait for them to change the words. I would think, *Man, when are they going to change this song?* Pentecostals can sing a chorus fifteen and sometimes twenty times.

For example, one time they started singing "I've got a feeling everything's going to be all right." That's the chorus: "I've got a feeling everything's going to be all right." Amen. Thirty minutes later, "I've got a

feeling...." I looked at my oldest brother and said, "I've got a feeling that's all they know."

So we started making jokes. We would start singing, "I've got a feeling they should learn some other songs. I've got a feeling we're going to be old and gray by the time this song's over." We couldn't figure out some of them, you know. They were alien to us.

They'd just sing, and pretty soon some of them would start dancing. We were lost when they started dancing. We didn't know what to do. And I can tell you, people who go to a bar or nightclub know how to dance better than most Pentecostals! If you're in a club, you know how to move. But you can't do it that way in church. You take a person who can dance in a club, put him in church and he's lost. All he can do in church is just stomp around a little bit. Stomp, stomp, stomp. They call that dancing in church.

They can't dance in most churches, but if you go to a black church, for example, man, they can move! They move like a glorified James Brown. We like the black churches better, because they're moving. The white people are still trying to get the beat. Stomp, stomp, stomp. White people are out there stomping, saying, "Catch me, catch me, I'm going out." Isn't that the truth?

All of this kidding aside—how many times have you gone home from a great service and found yourself still hungry for more of God? Why? Because you've been dieting on spiritual fasts for so many years that one service is not enough to quench the hunger and thirst in your heart. In fact, I don't think we'll ever be quenched within God's presence. We should always want more.

If you find yourself hungry for more of the Lord, then get into His presence. Get greedy for God. Begin to fellowship with Him until you're flowing with Him. Jesus said, **"Blessed are those who hunger and thirst for righteousness, for they shall be satisfied"** (Matt. 5:6 RSV). If you need more of the Lord, try drinking from the cup of the Lord's covenant instead of from religious cups. It will fill you up.

if, used often as a strong affirmative reply
"You lak to dance?" — **"If!"**

33

Salvation for a Cow

The first major revival I ever preached was in a Baptist church in Ladonia, Texas. I knew I'd reached the big time when I preached in a place like Ladonia. At that time, eight hundred and nine happy people welcomed you to that city when you drove in.

I'd never been there before, so I didn't know what to expect. Of course, I thought I was going to preach in a building. Well, that wasn't the way it was going to be, I found out later. We drove into town, and I saw this beautiful Baptist church with white pillars. I thought, *Praise God! Owww! Can these things be? Glory! I've hit the big time. I'm going to preach in a church with white pillars in front. Glory to God.*

I asked, "Is this where we're going to preach?"

"Uh, no," said the man driving me around. "No, not exactly."

"Not exactly?"

He told me I wasn't going to preach there. In fact, he told me I wasn't going to be preaching in a building at all. Instead, I was going to preach in a man's field.

"We're going to have a brush arbor meeting," he told me. "You're going to be preaching in a brush arbor revival."

"Where's Brush Arbor?" I asked. "I thought I was preaching in Ladonia. Now you're saying I'm preaching in Brush Arbor."

I didn't even know what a brush arbor was. I thought "brush arbor" was the name of the town: Brush Arbor, Texas. I'd never heard of a brush arbor before.

"The town is called Brush Arbor?" I asked.

"No, the name of the town is Ladonia."

"Well," I said, "where is Brush Arbor?"

"Oh," he said, "let me show you where brush arbor is."

We drove out to a cow pasture!

Out in the middle of this cow pasture was a bunch of sticks stuck into the ground, half cut, with chicken wire on top of them. On top of that was grass and tree limbs. This, I found out, was where I was going to be preaching. I was a little confused.

"What if it rains?" I asked.

"Well, you'll get wet."

"Oh," I said. "Well, praise God. Okay."

Now, you've got to understand, I'm a Cajun boy. Cajuns don't see much pastureland; Cajuns see swamps. That night, I was seeing pasture, man. I could see pasture everywhere—pasture and some cows.

"They've got cows out here," I commented.

"Yeah," he said. "The man who owns the field also owns the cows."

"Well, aren't you going to get the cows out of the pasture before I start to preach?" I asked.

"Well, no, we can't get the cows out because then we couldn't use the pasture," he told me.

"Well, suppose the cows come in when I'm preaching," I asked.

"Oh, they won't come in. They don't like people."

"Okay," I said, "You sure?"

"I'm sure," he said.

That was the first lying Baptist I ever met in my life! That night I went to preach out there in an 890-acre cow pasture, and all we had in the whole place were thirty-four people and a couple of cows. Thirty-four people and a couple of cows looked like an awfully small gathering in the middle of 890 acres of pastureland.

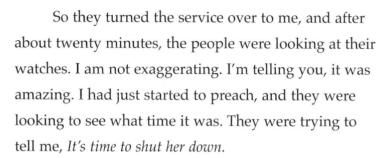

So they turned the service over to me, and after about twenty minutes, the people were looking at their watches. I am not exaggerating. I'm telling you, it was amazing. I had just started to preach, and they were looking to see what time it was. They were trying to tell me, *It's time to shut her down.*

So I started to wind it up, glory to God. I said, "Everybody, bow your heads and close your eyes." Boy, I was excited. I was ready for God to use me. God was going to use me, and I knew it. But I'll you what was really about to happen. God was about to fall off the throne with laughter.

I bowed my head along with everybody else. I told everybody, "Nobody look around." I had heard somebody say that once, and I thought it sounded really spiritual. So I used it at my meeting. "Bow your heads," I told those folks. "Nobody look around! If you don't know Jesus tonight, and you'd like to meet Him, I'm going to ask you right now, with every head bowed and every eye closed...."

I asked anyone who wanted to get saved to come on up and receive Jesus. My eyes were closed, so I didn't know who was coming. But all of the sudden I heard, "Moooooo!"

I opened my eyes and saw a great big cow standing at the altar! My first convert was going to be a cow! A cow came into that service to receive Jesus. People started laughing, but it was not funny. I wanted to quit preaching right there. I was so mad at God. I could just see God sitting on the throne and saying, *Look! A cow! Why, that boy's got power. He's got cows coming to the altar.*

I was so embarrassed. I was up there earnestly asking for people to get saved, and instead of people, I got a cow. The cow was up there just looking at me with blank eyes. He didn't know why he was up there.

"Can somebody get this cow out of here?" I asked.

I found out later that there was a reason that cow came up to receive Jesus. The very next week, they took that cow to the slaughterhouse. That's what the owner told me. I guess the cow had to get his life right before he went to meet his Maker.

I got back to where I was sleeping that night and thought I was such a failure, but the Lord told me, *Jesse, you obeyed me. You did what I asked you to, and I will honor it.* I preached there the next night and the night after that. All in all, I preached there a week, and those people blessed me. They really did. They blessed me.

God may have you do things that seem like
a failure to you, but with God it's not a failure. You
can't always see what God is doing behind the scenes
for you. The reason you don't always see God doing
something is not that He's being passive. He's waiting
for you to speak the Word. And when you step out on
the Word of God, He reveals what He's been doing
behind the scenes. He'll honor His Word when you're
faithful to proclaim it.

Jesse's Wife Cathy's Oyster and Artichoke Soup

    2 sticks butter
    2 large onions, finely chopped
    ¾ cup flour
    4 cups chicken broth
    2 cups milk
    *2 cans artichoke hearts in water, drained and
    mashed
    *2 quarts oysters in water
    generous amounts of spices to taste:
       basil

garlic powder
celery salt
lemon pepper
red pepper
thyme
salt and pepper
fresh parsley, chopped
fresh green onions, chopped

In large soup pot, sauté onions in butter. Add flour, and mix until it becomes a paste. Add chicken broth and milk, and mix together. Add remaining ingredients and cook on medium heat until oysters curl. Do not boil. Turn off heat and allow to set with lid on. Serve hot and enjoy!

*You may substitute these main ingredients for almost anything you can imagine:
    fresh mushrooms sautéed in butter and artichokes
    broccoli and cheese
    crab and cheese
    potato, bacon and cheese

Cathy's diet modification: In order to watch your carbohydrate intake, reduce the flour to ¼ cup, and instead of milk, add 2 cups of whipping cream.

34

Knock Him Down—and Repent Later!

As a kid, I remember my grandpa telling me, "Now, I know your mom and dad are into religion, but boy, if a man gets in your face, knock him down and repent later. Bust him in the head if he messes with you."

My grandpa used to tell me that. He would say, "Look, boy, don't take nothing off no one. Just knock his head off."

"But it's a sin," I would say.

"Well, repent later."

My mamma found out that my grandpa was telling me stuff like that, and she said, "Daddy, don't you tell Jesse to do that!"

"I don't want nobody beating up my grandson," he told her.

Grandpa came over to me after she left and said, "I'll tell you something, boy. If you get whipped, I'm going to whip you when you get home."

"Okay, Paw-paw," I said. "I ain't letting nobody whip me."

Sure enough, the next day some guy got in my face, and I hit him with a baseball bat. *Whack!* Down he went, Jack. I was fired up. When the teachers came to get me, I said, "You all want some of this? Come on! My Paw-paw said I'm supposed to repent in a few minutes, but right now I'm going to knock some heads."

I was in the seventh grade, and I got suspended for doing that. Well, why did I do it? I told everybody it was Paw-paw's fault.

My mamma beat the fire out of me. She went down there and begged the school to let me back in. My dad, on the other hand, was worried about how much it was going to cost. "What's the matter with you, boy!" he said. "Who's going to pay for this? I ain't paying for this, son." Then he turned to me and kind of smiled. He said, "Yeah, boy, you hit 'em with a bat! You knocked him down on one leg, didn't you? Yeah, I bet he went out like a light. That's my boy!"

"Don't glorify that," my mamma said.

"You shouldn't have done that, son," he said. My dad changed his mind.

When my grandpa heard what I had done at school that I'd been suspended for, he took me into the back-yard because he didn't want to say anything in front of Mamma. He told me he'd have done the same thing.

"Well, why didn't you stand up for me?" I asked him.

"I did, man," he said. "But you know I don't want to get involved in your family business."

"You almost got me killed, Paw-paw."

"Oh, you'll make it," he said. "Don't worry about it."

I always believed what my grandpa told me. Hey, if grandpa said do it, we did it. It's amazing how much influence your relatives can have over you. I had to be careful which one of my family members I listened to. All of them were telling me different things, and I had to figure out which was the right one.

That's why the Bible says in Mark 4:24 to take heed what you hear. Just like all those different people in my family telling me what to do, there are different voices in the world that will try to influence what you do. Only the godly voices are the right ones. You've

got to be sure that you're building your life on the wisdom of God; otherwise you can get into trouble, just like I did as a kid.

lak, to show affection
*"Ah **lak** her but she don **lak** me."*

35

THE DEMON-
POSSESSED
AiR TraveLER

Did you know that I've cast out devils on planes before? It's true. I didn't want to, but at the time I didn't have much choice. I was on a plane once when a woman walked past me and went, "Arghhhh," in a really deep voice. I heard that but never thought anything about it. People say strange things all the time, and mostly I just think, *That's okay, Jack, I'm minding my own business.*

Anyway, when this woman passed by, the Lord said, *Did you see that demon-possessed person?*

Yes, I did, I said under my breath.

What are you going to do about it? He asked.

Nothing, I said.

Why aren't you going to do something? He asked me.

Because, God, I said, *I'm on a plane!*

I know where you are, He said. *I'm talking to you. Don't you think I know where you are?*

But, God, I said, *I'm on a plane.*

I know you're on a plane, He said. *Are you going to let that person die and go to hell with that possessing spirit?*

Yeah, I said. *God, If I don't open my mouth up, I won't look like a preacher. I'll look like a businessman, not a preacher.* It's true. I've had people think I was a lawyer or a doctor. So I told God I didn't want to make all kinds of commotion on the plane.

Just then the woman with the devil in her got up and went back and sat down about four seats behind me. She had been in the wrong seat. I could hear her back there, and I could hear that spirit inside her. The Lord asked me again, *What are you going to do about that?*

I wasn't planning on doing anything, Lord, I said. *Look, God, this is a plane! If I do something about this devil, they're going to bring in a bunch of men in white coats to take me off this plane. That's what will happen if we start this stuff.*

He answered, *I didn't tell you to get up and go lay hands on the woman. You can rebuke that spirit right where you are.*

Sounds good to me, I said. *I can do that, God. It's not as embarrassing that way.*

So I got my seat buckled up, bless God, because I knew this thing was going to get hot. And under my breath I started saying, *You devil, demon from hell, I bind you. I bind you, in Jesus' name. I command you to loose that woman in Jesus' name!*

While I was doing this, I unintentionally started praying in tongues right there on the plane.

The guy sitting next to me looked over and asked, "Is there something wrong, buddy?"

"No, no, no," I said. "There's nothing wrong."

You know, I get expressive when I pray. I can't help it. I'm expressive. And I kept silently saying, *You demon devil! You've got the gall and audacity to growl at me? You demon, I bind you in the name of Jesus.*

All of a sudden, I heard this noise behind me: "Rechhhh, yeooowwwwww, yeoowoowowoow." This continued for a minute, and then I heard a man shout, "Flight attendant!" This was quickly followed by *ding, ding, ding.*

It was the man sitting next to the woman I was praying for, and he was freaking out. He was saying, "Flight attendant, this person…something's wrong."

I heard the flight attendant run back there and say, "Oh—she might be having a seizure."

Just then I spoke up and said, "No, she's not. She's got a demon in her."

I said that, and it was as if everybody collectively went, "Whoa!" Believe me, that statement got everybody's attention. You say, "She's got a demon," and people say, "Let me out of here. I am out of here! Demons?"

When I said that, the man sitting next to me got up too.

"There's a devil in that woman," I said.

The flight attendant went, "Huhhuhuhuhh! Well, what are we gonna do?"

At that point, I should have received an offering. I could've paid cash for everything right there on the plane with that offering and maybe even the plane, too, glory to God. But I didn't do that. I just said, "We're going to cast this devil out."

Everybody was looking at me now. I had definitely identified myself as a preacher by this time. There was no longer any doubt in anyone's mind that I was not a businessman. I started hollering at that devil. I shouted, "You devil from hell, I bind you, in Jesus' name!"

I heard, "Wauuuuughshhghghguuuu!" come out of that woman.

"Get out!" I shouted.

That woman groaned, "Auhhhhhhhhhhh!" and relaxed immediately.

"I think you killed her, man," the guy next to her said.

"No," I said, "I didn't kill her."

She was going through deliverance, and I was binding this devil, when all of a sudden the anointing to preach came on me. I stood up and looked at those people in that plane and said, "Let me tell you something! If you're not born again, that devil can jump all over this plane and get inside each and every one of you. Do you hear what I'm saying?"

Boy, by that time I was preaching. It was coming on me strong. I tell you what—I had the fire. We had Buddhists praying to God, sinners praying to God: "Oh, Jesus...." People had their beads out, going, "Hail, Mary...."

Everybody in that plane was praying!

Guess what? We cast that devil out! Afterward, that lady put her hand on mine and told me she had been in bondage since she was a small child. She thanked me for delivering her.

"Ma'am, don't thank me," I told her. "The Lord Jesus Christ did it."

After a while she finished talking, and I told her she was welcome, and we settled back down again. Then the guy seated next to me looked over and asked, "Uh, are there any more devils on this plane?"

"No," I said, "I don't see any."

"Ohhhh, thank God."

It was amazing. I had no idea God was going to use me like that on a plane. That's why you never know when there is going to be a ministry opportunity. But you always have to prepare like there's going to be one. The Bible says to preach the Word and be ready in and out of season. (2 Tim. 4:2.) It's amazing what opportunities will come up for you to preach the gospel and get people delivered, healed and set free.

Jesse's Sister-in-law Alma's Pecan Pie

- 1   cup light corn syrup
- 1   cup sugar
- 1½ cups pecans, chopped
- 2   tablespoons butter, melted
- 3   eggs slightly beaten
- 1   teaspoon vanilla
- 1   9-inch deep dish unbaked pie shell

In a large bowl, mix sugar and syrup together. Add eggs, vanilla and butter. Mix well. Stir in pecans. Pour mixture into unbaked pie shell. Bake at 325° for 50-60 minutes.

36

"I'LL TAKE THE GIDEON"

I gather you realize by now I have many airplane stories because I fly so much. I probably fly 300,000 to 350,000 miles a year preaching the gospel. Spending that much time on airplanes gives me great opportunities to be a witness for Jesus. I usually get the flight attendants to help me out with my witnessing. They come by with a magazine rack and ask passengers what magazine they would like to read. When they get to me, I always ask for the same thing. For example, I tell the flight attendant, "I'll take the Gideon."

One time when I said this, the flight attendant questioned me. "The *Gideon?*" she asked. She wasn't sure what I meant.

"Yes, the Gideon." I said.

"There's no magazine named the Gideon," she said.

"Oh, yes, there is," I said. "In fact, there's one here on this plane right now."

"We must have missed it," she said.

"No, it's there," I said. "You've just never picked it up. You've never offered it to anybody before. That's all."

"Well, what is the *Gideon?*" she asked me. "What does it look like?"

"Go back to the rack and look in there," I told her.

I saw the flight attendant go back and look in the magazine rack and read the words, "Placed by the Gideons."

She came back to me and said, "Oh, the Bible."

"Yes!" I said. "A Bible!"

She gave me the Bible, and I started reading from the beginning. I love Genesis, and it gets very vivid to me when I read it. So I turned that Gideon's Bible to page 1 and started reading. And in my mind I was reading Genesis 1:1,2, **In the beginning God created the heaven and the earth. And the earth was without form, and void; and darkness was upon the face of the deep. And** [*whirrrrrrrrrrrrrr*] **the spirit of God moved.** The word *moved* in the Hebrew means "fluttered."[1]

---

[1] Strong, "Hebrew," entry #7363, p. 108. (Strong, James. *Strong's Exhaustive Concordance of the Bible.* "Hebrew and Chaldee Dictionary," "Greek Dictionary of the New Testament." Nashville: Abingdon, 1890.)

Now, this was going on strong in my mind, and I got excited about it. I got so excited that the man sitting next to me started to notice.

I started saying, "Woowwwwwww! Glooooory!"

That man looked at me and asked, "What's the matter?"

I said, "God! He just created the earth! Look!"

He said, "Ooohhh. Man, you're really into this."

"No," I said, "it's into me."

"You seem really excited," he said.

"Yes, I am! I am possessed!"

That guy looked at me and went, "Whoaaaaa!" He wanted to know what planet I had come from.

He looked at me and said, "You must be religious."

"No, no," I said. "Religious people don't talk about God. Born-again people witness about God. Religious people have Thursday night visitations, a time when they walk up to people's homes at dinnertime and say, `Hello, would you like to join my religion and become just like me?' No, I don't think so. Religion is very boring. But I'm very expressive when I talk about the Lord because I enjoy Jesus."

I shook this man up, and I knew it. I knew I could preach to him on that airplane because he wasn't going anywhere. I've never seen anyone yet

with enough faith to get off an airplane which was going 500 miles an hour. If they do get up and run, they can only go so far, you know. If they try to escape to the bathroom, for example, you can just get on the microphone and get to them in there.

So I witnessed to this man right there on the airplane. Sometimes God's Word will become so alive to you that you can't help witnessing. It will just fill you up inside until you feel as if you're going to burst unless you say something. You can actually get so full of God's Word that you feel like you must talk to somebody about Jesus or you'll burst.

That's the creative power of the Holy Spirit. As you exalt Jesus, the Holy Spirit will begin to flutter just like He did in Genesis when God was creating the earth. That's the creative factor of the Trinity. God's just waiting for you to get excited about Him. Then the minute you start talking about Jesus, it's like saying, "Light, be!" It will cause the Holy Spirit to flutter on the heads of people and create an atmosphere for them to get born again into the kingdom of Jesus Christ!

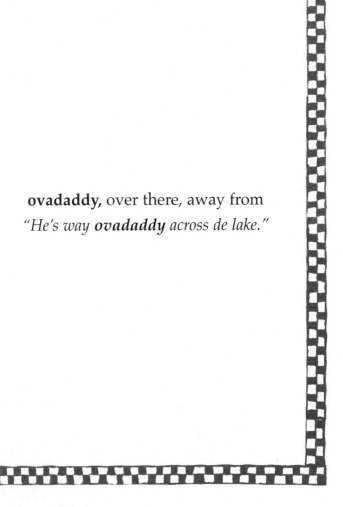

ovadaddy, over there, away from
*"He's way **ovadaddy** across de lake."*

37

LOST iN LA

Did you know that I once got lost in downtown Los Angeles in the middle of the night? It's true; I really got lost in the middle of downtown LA! I had just preached a meeting and was being driven into downtown Los Angeles at about midnight when my driver and I got lost. I don't know how it was possible for us to get lost there, but we did it.

I looked around and saw all these burned-out buildings, and I thought, *My God! I'm in the middle of a riot.* These two kids came up to the car and asked us if we knew where we were. I told them that I had no idea where we were, and then I asked them if they knew. They didn't even know where *they* were. They said they'd never been there before, but they thought it was where all the riots started.

Then I started to look around. I saw all these tough-looking guys dressed up like gang members. They kind of looked like that RCA dog, but with their caps on sideways. My first thought was that they were going to look into my car and see me with this suit on and try to rob me.

Just then my driver said, "Brother Jesse, I don't know where we are, but I'm going to pull over. You get out of the car and go ask those guys where the airport is."

Yeah, right! I reminded him who he was talking to. I said, "I'm the guest speaker. I'm not supposed to get killed. There are gangs out there!"

"Yeah," he said, "but, Jesse, you've got more faith than I have."

"No, I don't," I said. "I ain't going out there and asking them where we are."

But I asked the Lord what He thought I should do, and I heard Him tell me that I would be okay. So I decided to go ask those tough-looking guys where we were. The first thing I did when I opened that door was to let them know who I was. They noticed me the second I got out of that car. I didn't wait for them to start saying anything; instead, I just started shouting, "Glory! Hallelujah! Thank You, Jesus. Hallelujah!"

I shouted every kind of praise word I could think of to let them know I was a child of God. I just started saying, "Glory, hallelujah! Where's the

airport?" You have to realize, I was talking to gang members in downtown LA in the middle of the night.

They heard me shouting stuff about Jesus and the airport and just kind of looked at me funny for a minute. Then one of them said, "Yeah, go down that road, turn two blocks later, go a mile and a half and you'll run into it."

"God bless you!" I shouted. "So long."

I got back into the car and looked over my shoulder as we drove off. They were saying something to each other, and I could just imagine what it was. I could almost tell what they were thinking by the looks on their faces. They were going, *Why didn't we steal that car? That man's got white hair, a briefcase and a suit. He's got money!*

But the Lord protected us. I went into a dangerous place and got out safely. Why did that happen? It happened because God told me I'd be safe and because I came out of the car praising God. I let them know I was a Christian. I didn't come out of the car and say, "Would you like to meet Jesus Christ as Lord of your life? I'm a Methodist." If I would've said that—*boom!*—they probably would've shot me.

"Hi, I'm a Baptist."

Boom!

"Hello, I'm a Pentecostal Holiness preacher."
Boom!

I didn't say any of those things. I just got out praising God, and I believe it scared them.

That's what you have to do in dangerous situations. You've got to come out blasting praises with both barrels. Fire back at danger with a weapon stronger than any danger you could ever face. Praising God releases His power to protect and shelter you in the middle of any storm you might face.

Do you remember what God's army, the Israelites, did in their battles? Look at the battle at Jericho, for example. The Israelites didn't even raise a spear against the enemy. They shot no arrows and used no swords—they used the weapon of praise. After walking in silence six times around that fortified city of Jericho, they started shouting and hollering and praising God. Glory, hallelujah! Every obstacle in their path was totally destroyed by the praises of God.

And God's given you that same power against any danger you might face. So the next time you're in trouble, shout praises to God!

Jesse's Sister-in-Law Christine's Pecan Pralines

3 cups sugar
1 large can of evaporated milk
1 can of sweetened condensed milk
4 tablespoons butter
3 cups pecans
1 teaspoon vanilla

In a 6-quart pot, add butter, sugar, evaporated and condensed milk. Cook on medium heat until thick and bubbly, stirring continually while cooking. Once the mixture is thick and bubbly, you can test it by dropping ¼ teaspoon into a glass of cold water. If done, it should form a soft, firm ball when dropped into the water. When the candy reaches this consistency, add the pecans and vanilla and continue cooking until it returns to the same thick and bubbly consistency. Do another sample test.

Once the candy is ready, remove from heat and spoon onto the slick side of buttered freezer paper.

Depending on how big you make each praline, this recipe should yield about 20-24 candies.

38

CRYING CaTHY

God uses my wife, Cathy, in mysterious ways. It's so mysterious I don't even understand it. All I know is that my wife has been given the ministry of tears. She can't open her mouth to preach a sermon without crying. She gets very emotional when she preaches. Let me tell you what I mean.

I got a call one day to do a television interview, and I asked Cathy to go along with me.

"I don't want to go," she told me.

"Come on," I said.

"But they want to talk to you," she said.

"Well, talking to me is talking to you," I explained. "Come on. I want you to be with me on the program."

"I don't want to go," she insisted.

Man, she was reluctant. I had to drag her onto that program with me, but I finally got her to go. She sat right there on stage with me as they interviewed me. They asked me to go over my testimony and

explain how the Lord delivered me from my heathe-
nistic lifestyle and got me into the ministry. I started
talking about it, and before you knew it, I was preaching. I had the Holy Ghost working through me, and I
was preaching the gospel to those people.

After a while the host of the show said, "Isn't
that wonderful? People in the television audience, I
want you to get on your phone and call if you're being
touched by the power of God." Then he turned to me
and said, "Now, you have your lovely wife with you."

"Yes," I said, "this is my wife, Cathy."

He turned to Cathy and asked, "Cathy, would
you please tell us how it happened that you got saved
before Jesse did? What happened?"

Now, I knew that Cathy usually didn't preach
without crying. So I was ready to see her start crying,
but I had no idea that everyone connected with the
whole show was going to start bawling too. Cathy
started talking about how the Lord had come into her
life, and sure enough—*Boo hoo, hoo*—she started to cry.

I looked over and saw Cathy crying, and it made
me cry! I started going, "Oh, bububububububu."
Now Cathy was crying, I was crying and *then* the host
started crying! He just looked over at the two of us

blubbering away and started crying himself. He forgot all about me.

Once that happened, the phones started ringing off the wall. People were being touched. It was wonderful. That precious gift of tears from the Holy Ghost went right through that camera and into the homes of the people who were watching.

For example, one woman called and told Cathy she would share her heart with Cathy because Cathy had gotten that heathen of a husband saved. At that point, my tears stopped, and I said, "Wait a minute, ma'am. I used to be a heathen, but I'm not a heathen anymore."

"Yeah," she said, "but I don't doubt there's some traces of it still in your life."

"All right," I said, "it's time to take the next call."

We had fun that day watching the Lord use Cathy to minister to people. Like I said, He always used tears during Cathy's sermon to get through to people. Well, that was about to change.

I'll never forget the first time Cathy preached a full sermon. It was a blessing, because it was a shock to me and everyone else. One day Cathy came to me and said, "I'm going to preach without crying!"

I thought, *Praise God. I've got to see this. Hallelujah! She's crossed her Jordan. She's possessing the land!*

Cathy made up her mind to preach a full-length sermon without tears, and she did! She went out there and "jumped across the Jordan." The Hittites were there, but she just kept going. She started preaching a mile a minute. She said, "I want to tell you what God said…and I want you to turn to the book of Genesis… and Jesus…I want to tell you, He's Lord…!"

Now, my wife doesn't usually talk fast. In fact, I talk a lot faster than she does, but when she started to preach that day, she talked at lightening speed. She talked so fast that she preached an hour's sermon in two minutes. And when she was done, she stopped and said, "Now that's the truth!" It had authority.

I heard that and thought, *Who was that? Was that my wife? Hey, let's go back a few verses because I missed something. Did that get on tape?*

It was too fast!

"We tried to get it on tape," the tape guys said, "but it was too fast."

Afterward, Cathy was concerned about her delivery. Naturally, she wanted to know she did well, but it had nothing to do with that delivery. I want you to get the point. It had nothing to do with delivery. What

Cathy said in those few minutes changed people's lives. God supernaturally sped up people's hearing. The audience went, *Wrrrr, werrrrr—yeah. I got it!* It was powerful.

As a result of that message from the Holy Ghost, people came to the altar, bawling and squawling, and got saved like never before. I heard one person say, "That's the way I like preaching. You can understand it."

It was a miracle. God moved on Cathy's heart, and she entered into a new flow. That's why you can never get bored with the Holy Ghost. The Holy Ghost won't always minister the same way every time. But if you're bored with the gospel, and if the Bible is stale to you, then you need a refreshing. Ask God to open up his Word to you and make it alive to your heart. Don't ever let the Bible get old. Learn to expect surprises from God that will bless you.

pooyie, distasteful, offensive
*"You smelled dat perfume
she has on."* ***"Pooyie!"***

39

HEAVEN AT THE BEST STOP

I face one of the hardest temptations in the world every time I go to Lake Charles, Louisiana. When I get on interstate 10, I can almost smell the cooking from Best Stop. Best Stop is a restaurant with some of the best Cajun cooking in the state. Dear God, they've got boudin like you ain't never eaten in your life. In case you don't know what boudin is, it's a Cajun sausage with cooked rice mixed right into the stuffing. It's plain good eating!

When you walk into that restaurant, you can just smell the cholesterol. I mean, that food will kill you, but you'll die with a smile on your face. Every time we stop there, it's Cathy's fault. Whenever we get near that place, she says, "Jesse, let's get us some boudin."

"Oh, Cathy," I say, "don't tempt me, woman. That temptation is talking to me."

You see, I love to eat cholesterol. I like hog cracklings, hogshead cheese, and hot boudin. I love boudin. I want the grease, man. I want it where you've got to use Bounty extra-strength paper towels just to hold on to it.

Best Stop has the kind of food I'm talking about. Every time we go in there, everyone looks so content. They're so happy eating that grease. You don't see people like that at health food stores. If you go into a health food store, for example, the people you see aren't happy. They look like they have bulimia, and they're anorexic. They're drinking powdered drinks, and they're too thin. Not at Best Stop, boy. I go to the Best Stop, and those bellies are hanging over every-where. I tell those folks that the food they're eating will kill them, and they say, "Yeah, so what? It tastes good."

Actually, you know, I heard of people who ate Cajun food like that all of their lives and lived to be ninety-eight years old. (Of course, they might have lived to be a hundred and forty if they hadn't eaten all the grease they had!)

Best Stop is not a fancy place, you understand. It doesn't make any difference who you are. Employees in there will just go, "What you need, huh?" when you're trying to buy something to take home. They sell the ingredients for Cajun cooking, too, but nobody in there is going to get them for you. You can get them yourself.

For example, if you're looking for some particular product, they'll just say, "Go down that aisle and look there."

You may be yelling, "Down here?" from across the room.

They'll just holler back, "Look past the Brawny stuff. Yeah, you see it?"

"No."

"You want me to come over there?" they're hollering from the front.

"No, I got it. Thank you."

It doesn't matter if you can't find what you need. Everybody who goes in there has to look for what they need.

When my wife gets into Best Stop, she changes from a beautiful, elegant woman to a down-home Cajun. When it comes time to eat boudin, all of a sudden, that Cajun from the Bayou comes out, and she gets down to her roots, man. She comes alive when she sees those hot boudin links. I can see it come upon her. She loves to eat that boudin!

And there's a certain way you have to eat boudin. To eat it like a true Cajun, you've got to tear it apart with your teeth. You see, it's sausage that comes in links. That means, sometimes you've got to work at it to get those links torn apart. You've got to put one end in your mouth and pull the other end with you hands while you're going, "Ouh, orgggg, ohhhhgm pull, pull!" You might even need someone to help you pull at the other end to get it apart.

Cathy eats that stuff up. She will eat her links of boudin and then wash it down with a diet soda. She really will! She will eat that greasy Cajun sausage and then still wash it down with some diet soda. Usually she turns to me and asks me if I want some too.

Can you see me trying to eat some boudin and drive at the same time? It's hard enough to eat boudin in a restaurant. But when you eat it in the car, you've got to turn loose and eat with both hands. And if I've got boudin all over my face, I don't care that I'm doing sixty-five miles an hour down the interstate. I'll grab a link and start tearing at it while keeping one greasy hand on the steering wheel. Cathy will help me by grabbing the other end of the link with both hands, trying to tear it apart.

You can see the headline now, *Television evangelist killed with a piece of boudin in his mouth.*

Some of you—especially you up North—are still trying to figure out what boudin is. It ain't tongues, boy. It's Cajun sausage. Try some. You'll like it.

Now you may be asking yourselves, *What does boudin have to do with God?* Boudin doesn't have anything to do with God! I'm trying to get you to laugh. I know exactly what I'm doing.

"What are you saying, Brother Jesse?" you may ask. I'm saying you need to laugh. There's enough junk in the world that will depress you. For example, it's not funny when you see kids on drugs. It's not funny when husbands or wives run out on each other. It's not funny when people are messing up their lives and doing terrible things. It's a lost and dying world out there.

I'll do whatever it takes to get through to desperate people. I'll do whatever it takes to glorify Jesus. Sometimes telling a story about some greasy old boudin is the best way to get folks to stop thinking about their problems. When they laugh, I can get them to a place where I can minister to them. That's the way you've got to be with troubled people. Make them laugh, and then slip some of Jesus in on them.

Jesse's Sister-in-law Christine's Punch Bowl Cake

1 package angel food cake
3 containers fresh (or, if not in season, frozen)
   strawberries
4 bananas
1 large can of crushed pineapple in heavy syrup
1 large box of instant vanilla pudding
1 medium container whipped topping
   optional: 1 cup chopped pecans or walnuts

Wash the strawberries and set aside 7 of the most attractive to use as a garnish. Be sure to leave the stems on.

In a mixing bowl, slice the remaining strawberries into thin slices. Then slice the bananas and add to the strawberries. Add the can of crushed pineapple with the syrup. Mix well. Refrigerate for 1 hour to allow the fruit mixture to blend together.

While the fruit mixture is setting up, prepare the vanilla pudding according to the directions on the box. Fold in the whipped topping. Place mixture in the refrigerator and allow to set for 15-30 minutes.

Slice the angel food cake into at least 15 slices.

In a large punch bowl, layer the fruit mixture, cake (5 slices per layer) and pudding mixture. Repeat layering 3 times, ending with the pudding mixture on the top.

Garnish with the whole strawberries. Refrigerate at least 1 hour before serving.

*Optional: If you like nuts, you can add this to the layering. You can use chopped pecans or walnuts. Just add them on top of the fruit mixture while layering. You can also sprinkle a few on the top before you add the strawberries.

40

STORIES OF MY CRAZY FIRST EMPLOYEE

You must believe something good about every-one, because no one is hopeless. Every person you meet has some value. Now, I've had some people working for me who I *thought* were hopeless. Let me tell you, some of these people were seriously hopeless-looking people. I looked at some of these people and thought, *God, I wouldn't want to hire these people to work for me.* Let me just give you a prime example.

I hired a guy over sixteen years ago who still works with me today. He was my very first ministry employee besides Cathy. When I first hired him, his pastor told me, "Don't hire that boy." That's what he told me! So I agreed not to until I heard the Lord tell me otherwise. But sure enough, God said, *Hire him.*

"Oh, Jesus!" I said. "God, did you hear what his pastor said?" God answered me and said, *What his pastor said is the truth. But hire him anyway, and I will perfect him through your ministry.*

That's how I came to hire this guy. As soon as he started working for me, he jumped in with both feet. He would say, "Tell me what to do, boss, and I'll do it for you. I'll do anything for you!"

"Thank you," I'd say. "Just do your job. That's all we want you to do."

"I'll do that!"

Now, the Bible says that in your patience you possess your soul. (Luke 21:19.) Well, I possessed my soul three or four times over with this boy. He did some of the craziest things you have ever seen in your life. For example, he was driving one of our ministry vans with Cathy one night, and I was up ahead in another car. It was late, and Cathy asked him to drive a little faster so they could stay with me and the others.

He turned to Cathy and said, "Yeah—if the Lord tells me to, Sister Cathy, I will."

Oh, that made Cathy mad. She was just steaming! Steaming! She told me later, "Fire that sucker!"

Later I had a talk with that boy about that. I said, "Boy, come here! Listen, you are causing my wife to get

on my back. If you keep her off my back, I will stay off your back. Do you understand? Let me give you some wisdom. Shut your mouth when you're in the car with Cathy. If she tells you to drive 95, drive 95. If you get a ticket, we'll pay for it. If she tells you to do something, do it. Did you ever hear what Jesus' mother said? She said, 'Whatever He tells you to do, do it.'"

That was the first little mistake he made with Cathy. But there were others. I don't know what was wrong with him. For example, he would look at Cathy and say, "Boy, your hair is ugly today, Sister Cathy."

I heard that, and I told him, "Look, speak in tongues. Don't speak in English anymore!"

He didn't tell her that to be rude; he just said whatever came to his mind. Let me tell you what I'm talking about. One time we were in a pastor's house having dinner, and the pastor turned to him and said, "Boy, you're a good worker."

He looked at the pastor and said, "Yeah, well, thank you. I appreciate it. But I couldn't work for you. You don't have any faith. Look at that trashy car you've got in your garage."

I couldn't believe it! This guy just spoke his mind! He didn't give any thought to the way it sounded. The Lord had some work to do on this guy.

I remember something that happened involving his car one time. You see, he drove a car that didn't have glass in the back window of the convertible, and he often used that car for the ministry. He once had my tape bag with my money in it and left it in the back seat of that car! When I asked him where the tape bag was, he told me, "I left it in the car."

"What?" I said. "You don't have a back window in your car!"

"The Lord will take care of it," was all he said.

"No," I said. "Get yourself up and go get that tape bag!"

Another time, something crazy happened with him during dinner at another pastor's house. The pastor's little boy was kind of messing with him at the dinner table. You know how kids can get. Well, after putting up with this for awhile, he told the boy, "Come here, little fellow. I want to talk to you for a minute."

He got up with the little boy—a five-year-old—and went out of the room. I thought, *Where's he going?* I heard them walk down the hall, and then I heard, *Whack! Whack!* My employee was spanking that pastor's little boy because he was messing with him!

He'd set his mind like that sometimes. I remember the time that he started thinking television was a sin. I don't know who told him that, but he became convinced that television was sin. So one day he went over to his mamma's house while she was watching a show and unplugged the television set. I think he thought he was being spiritual. But this was the way Fritz acted when he first started working for us.

"Look," I said once, "I don't want my battery running down on my battery pack. Make sure I have a new battery. Got it?"

"Okay, boss," he said. He never called me Jesse. He always called me boss: "Okay, *boss*. Whatever you say, *boss*. I got it, *boss*."

I asked him later, "Did you change my batteries? Do I have a new one?"

"You've got a new battery, boss," he said.

"What did you do with the old battery?" I asked him.

"I have it in my pocket," he said.

"Okay," I said. "Well, I'll see you tonight."

"Okay."

On the way to the meeting that night, the associate pastor asked me, "Brother Jesse, is it all right if I ride with your tape guy to the meeting tonight?"

"Sure," I said and told this employee to pick up the associate pastor.

So he got in the van and started driving down the road with the associate pastor, when suddenly his leg began burning. But instead of checking his own leg, he looked over at the associate pastor and said, "The Lord is telling me that you have a pain in your leg."

The associate pastor looked at him and said, "What?"

"I'm telling you," he said more strongly, "you have a pain in your leg!"

Then he slammed on the brakes, jumped out and started running around the van. The associate pastor got out of the van, thinking, *What is wrong with this crazy guy?*

Meanwhile, my tape guy is running around the van, thinking he's got a manifestation of the associate pastor's pain in the leg!

What had happened was that there was a penny in his pocket and it reacted with the battery, burning a hole in his skin. But he thought it was a word of knowledge from God for the associate pastor! That boy did some crazy things like that.

I'll give you another example of what I'm talking about. I came walking in the back door to a meeting we were having one time, and I saw him going, "Ohhh, ohhh," and shaking his head and pacing around.

I asked, "Do you have a problem? Is something wrong?"

"I'll tell you what," he said. "These women are lusting for me, Brother Jesse."

"What?" I said. "A grasshopper wouldn't lust for you, boy! For God's sake! They just want to be nice and say hello to you."

"No," he went on. "I can see it! They're lusting for me."

"You can't see nothing! Just sell the tapes!"

He thought that just because a woman was nice to him, it meant she lusted after him.

One time, I saw him leave the tape table and take off running at full speed. This was just after a big meeting, in which we'd had about fifteen hundred people. I saw him running like crazy right through the middle of them. I mean, he was going full blast. He is six feet three inches tall, and he weighs about a hundred and five pounds—skinny as a rail. He ran and tackled a guy in the middle of that room in front of everyone!

I thought, *My God! What is going on here?*

Everybody freaked out while he wrestled with the guy and took something from him. Then he came walking back over to the tape table, where told me, "I got it back! I got our tape back, boss."

He had tackled a guy in the middle of a church reception over a three-dollar tape that the man had stolen! That's the kind of person I was dealing with back then. This guy was a zealot. He couldn't be stopped when he thought something was wrong or out of place. That turned out to be a good quality later, but it needed to be perfected first.

Today this man is one of the finest men of God you will ever meet. He's been with me for over sixteen years, and he's done everything in the world for me. He's a servant who loves God. I could put my life in his hands, and my life wouldn't hit the ground. Why? Because he is a true servant of the Lord Jesus Christ. But we had to perfect that in him. It was in there, but somebody had to get it out. He didn't start out being such a blessing to us at all. During his first four years with us, I had to have the patience of Job.

You see, you must believe in everyone, because no one is hopeless. You can't look at someone and think, *He's hopeless,* or *She'll never amount to anything.* You don't know what their potential is, because you can't always see people the way God sees them. God looks at them through the eyes of faith. He knows what they're capable of becoming with a little patience and training.

Just look at the life of Moses. The same Moses who led millions of people out of Egypt, through the wilderness and to the Promised Land started out saying that he was slow of speech and slow of tongue. (Ex. 4:10.) But it was that same Moses who later talked freely with God and was a great leader.

That's why you can't judge a person by what they seem like to you at the time. God may be raising you up to train them or impart something to them, and one day you will look at them and say, "Man, just look at what you've become!"

---

salse, a seasoned preparation usually containing tomatoes, onions, garlic, etc.
"Clovis is cleaning de turtles,
you can start wit de salse."

41

TROUBLE WITH PANTYHOSE

I think whoever invented control-top pantyhose for women was a genius. That person must be rich, too, because almost every woman wants to buy those things. Incidentally, have you ever noticed that the women who buy those are also the ones who need them the worst? Let me tell you what I'm talking about.

I've been in the department store when women are trying on clothes, and I can always tell the ones wearing control tops. I could be all the way at the front of the store, and I'd still hear the sounds of a woman trying to get her control tops straightened out: *Snap, snap, pow!* She's grunting and groaning, trying to get her big rear end fitting right into this little, bitty stocking. Some women really get a workout, man.

But once she gets that control top in place and slides that dress on, look out! Here she comes out of

the dressing room, saying, "Look, honey. How do you like it?" Her husband doesn't even have a chance to answer, because all of a sudden a run starts busting up the front of those stockings. It looks like a tumor bursting out from underneath.

I think it's funny myself. Have you ever seen how itty bitty those control tops are without the woman in there?

How does she ever get herself into something so tiny? I don't know, but you can tell when it's over. It will pop like a shotgun when it doesn't work. She needs a healing in her waistline when it goes wrong. And if it does go on without running and bursting, it usually doesn't fit quite right. She starts walking funny, like those hose have gotten something caught in them that she's trying to get out. She's walking around kicking at the air, trying to loosen things up. Then she grabs at the control top and starts pulling on it. Tell me how you are not going to notice something like that?

Those things shouldn't be called control tops at all. To be truly correct, they should be called control bottoms. That's where women gain the weight! The difference between a woman and a man gaining weight is that a man gains it in the front, whereas a woman gains it in the back.

When you look at an overweight woman and say, "Boy, it looks like you gained a little weight there, huh, Mamma?" She may say, "Where? I don't see anything?" Of course she can't see it! All of it's trailing back behind her! She'll be walking and knocking things over, and she can't even see why. *Crash! Bam!* "Ooops, sorry," she says.

Another thing, you can always tell a woman is wearing control tops by how they look on her knees. The threads are bare up around the kneecaps because every time she goes to sit down, the thing gets stressed out. Her knees bend in those control tops, the threads start to bust and her skin turns all white because there's no blood coming into it. Sometimes, all that's holding the fat back is a few threads! You think, "Boy, if that sucker splits, it's going to kill us all."

I love to notice things like this about people. In fact, I just love watching people. People are so hilarious, and they don't even know it. They're just living their lives, and they don't even know that they're unique creatures.

I love people. They constantly amaze me. When I look at all the different kinds of people there are, it just fills me with awe for what God has created. God said that it was good when He sat back and looked at His creation, but I think that was an understatement. I think people are great—exploding control tops and all. Don't you?

Jesse's Mother-in-Law Irene's Rice Dressing

2 pounds lean pork
1 pound ground beef
1 pound chicken liver
1 pound chicken gizzards
2 large onions, chopped
¼ cup cooking oil
2 cups green onions, chopped
2 cups parsley, chopped
3 cups cooked rice
    salt and pepper to taste

Cut pork, liver and gizzards into small pieces. Brown onions in oil until medium brown. Add pork, liver and gizzards. Cook for 1 hour, stirring frequently. Add water if needed. Add ground beef, and cook for an additional 30 minutes. Add seasoning, and cook for another 20 minutes. When cooked, mash thoroughly with potato masher. Pour meat mixture into a large bowl, and add rice a little at a time until well blended.

Serves approximately 12.

42

WET PajaMaS

I haven't always slept in luxury rooms while on the road preaching. In fact, when I first got into the traveling ministry, I slept wherever there was an opening. Sometimes it was a blessing, and other times it wasn't. For example, I had a preacher tell me he wanted me to stay with him at his home one time. He had a nice home, and I was glad to stay with him because I didn't have any money to go to a hotel. He had a nice family with a little boy and girl who both really liked me.

Well, I went to sleep that night, and I slept hard like I always do. Cathy says when I sleep, a tornado could come flying through the room and I wouldn't ever wake up. When I sleep, I'm out cold, man. I'm just plain unconscious. That's the way I slept when I was at this man's house that night. Only this time I found out that something strange had happened in the night.

The next morning I woke up at about 7 A.M., and I felt something strange in the bed with me. When I looked over, I saw that the man's little boy and girl had come into the room and crawled into bed with me during the night without my knowing it had happened. Like I said, when I'm asleep, I'm sound asleep. One of those kids was on the left side of me, and the other was on my right. I thought, *What are these two kids doing in this bed with me?* But I didn't have too much time to find out the answer, because I noticed something even stranger than that.

As I became more aware of what had happened, I also became aware that I felt something strange on my leg. And when I looked under the covers to see what it was, I saw yellow water running down my body. *Oh, man,* I thought, *these kids went to the bathroom all over me!*

That's really what happened, but the kids didn't even know it. They woke up and saw me looking at my leg, and they said in unison, "We love you, Brother Jesse."

The parents came in about that time and said, "You all leave Brother Jesse alone! Come on, get up out of there and leave him be."

As soon as those kids got out of bed with me, their parents knew what had happened. That boy's pajama pants were all wet and hanging down, and the little girl's nightgown was all wet. When I got up, my pajamas were all wet and hanging down too.

"Oh no, did you two wet the bed again?" their parents asked. "Did they wet the bed on you, Brother Jesse?" *No kidding!*

That night the preacher told all the people in his congregation that his kids went to the bathroom all over Brother Jesse. "Brother Jesse's a humble man," he told them. "He didn't even get mad." That's right, I didn't get all upset over that situation. It doesn't pay to get all offended when little things happen to you, because offenses can tear apart good relationships.

Don't hold grudges against anyone. I don't care who they are or what they did—holding a grudge against someone will not hurt that person; it will only hurt you. Jesus said, **Woe unto the world because of offences! for it must needs be that offences come; but woe to that man by whom the offence cometh!** (Matt. 18:7).

Here Jesus was warning us of the danger of letting offenses take hold on your life. It's like poison in your heart.

Instead of getting offended and holding a grudge, just give it to Jesus and let it go. You'll be glad you did!

swimps, edible crustacean
common in South Louisiana
"Don forget de **swimps** *fo*
de gumbo tomorrow."

43

Smelly Bed, Angry Dog

I was sleeping at someone else's house while I was on the road preaching another time, and these people slept in total darkness. That man told me that his family didn't like any light coming through the windows at all when they slept.

"Brother Jesse," he asked me, "do you like to sleep in pitch darkness?"

"Yeah," I said. "It doesn't make any difference to me." I don't care how dark it is as long as I can get a good night's sleep. So that night he offered to let me use his son's bedroom, and I got hardly any sleep at all.

Here's what happened. First of all, I went into the son's room and turned on the light to make sure there wasn't anybody in there. When I looked around, I saw that everything looked fine, but I noticed that things didn't smell so good. And as soon as I got into

that kid's bed, I knew why. They must not have changed that kid's sheets in months. I mean, those sheets didn't smell too clean. They smelled like that boy.

I tried to get used to the smell. I cut the light out and tried to go to sleep. With the light out, it was so dark I couldn't see my own hand right in front of my face. It was pitch black, and all of a sudden I felt a tongue on my hand in the dark.

What! I thought. *What kind of creatures do they have living in here?* Well, I found out it was that kid's dog who had come up to sleep with me. He probably thought I was that kid. He jumped up in bed, and I could feel him flop down, but I couldn't see anything because it was so dark in there.

There I was in the middle of a pitch-black, smelly room, with a dog that I couldn't see on that bed with me. He was trying to lick me, and I was knocking things over with my hands, trying to find the lamp. When I finally did turn the light on, the dog saw that I wasn't the kid he thought he was smelling in that room. The dog couldn't smell me because all could he smell was that stinking kid whose bed I was sleeping in. Once he knew I was not the kid, he took one look at me, growled and started chewing on my face!

It didn't take long for me to do what I had to do. I took that dog and threw it up against the wall! I wasn't going to let a dog chew on my face. After I threw that dog against the wall, he got mad. He got up and started chasing me around the room. I was running all over the place, jumping over the bed and such, with this dog chasing after me!

All that noise must've awakened the man in his bedroom, because I heard him shouting something at me through the wall. I heard him telling me to kick the dog in the head. "Kick him!" he yelled. "Kick that dog in the head!"

After that instruction, I told that dog to go ahead and get bad with me if he wanted to. "Come on!" I shouted at him. He jumped up, and I swung back my leg. *Boot!* Boy, I kicked that dog good. He yelped and hit the floor flat on his back on the other side of the room.

For a minute I thought I might have killed that dog. But when I walked over to see if he was all right, he looked up and snapped at me.

"Yeah, you're all right!" I said.

I went through all kinds of these things during my early ministry. I prayed, "Lord, why must I suffer like this?"

Well, you didn't get bitten, He said. Then He said, *Jesse, I appreciate that you are willing to do anything, go anywhere—even sleep anywhere—for Me.*

Then I told Him that I didn't particularly care to suffer these things. And He told me that He didn't care for me to suffer that stuff either.

They should have treated you better, and I'll hold them accountable for it, He told me. *But you just preach the Word of God, and I'll take care of you.*

And He will too. God remembers all the sacrifices you have to make for Him in life. He's keeping track of the way people treat you, and He's going to reward you for bearing it. The Bible says that God keeps every one of your tears in a bottle. (Ps. 56:8.) So if God can keep track of all your tears, don't you think He sees all the little things you go through? He certainly does, and one day He will reward you openly for your sacrifices.

Jesse's Sister-in-Law Christine's Roux

1 cup unsifted all-purpose flour
1 cup vegetable oil

A roux is a mixture of equal amounts of flour and oil cooked until it is very brown with nut-like flavor and aroma. It is used for thickening many Cajun and French dishes, such as gumbo, sauce piquante, stews and sauces. Once you master this procedure, you will be successful in making Cajun dishes that require a roux.

Pour the amount of oil and flour that your recipe calls for into a heavy saucepan. Stir to a smooth paste. Cook over medium to medium-high heat, stirring constantly to prevent burning, until the mixture becomes golden or deep brown. A good roux usually takes 15 to 30 minutes to make.

The above measurement is a good standard for making a roux. If you are making a large gumbo or stew or any other Cajun dish that requires a roux, you may need to adjust this measurement. Remember to always refer to the ingredient list, and use the amount that is needed for your recipe.

44

ADulterous Churchgoers

One time I got so mad at God. He made me say something in the middle of my preaching that I never would've said on my own in a million years. I was preaching loud and hard in Vacherie, Louisiana, and I kept walking back and forth in front of these two couples on the front row. My God, it was a Holy Ghost night!

I was preaching away and walking and back and forth in front of these two couples, and then I just stopped. Now, as I said, I would *never* do what I did next, but God fooled me. He made it come out of my mouth before my mind could hear what I said. I looked at one of those women on the front row and said, "You, lady, are committing adultery with that man right there!"

Well, the pastor jumped up and said, "Oh, let's pray here! Let's pray!"

I stopped preaching, and everybody looked at me. All I could think was, *Get me out of here now!* I couldn't believe I had just accused these people of committing adultery! But I knew the voice of God, and I knew what I told that woman was from Him.

That woman and her husband both jumped to their feet in shock. Then the man that I had pointed to jumped to his feet. Three of them were standing by then—only the man's wife remained seated—and all four of them were looking straight at me. I didn't say another word. The only sound we could hear was the pastor's prayer language coming from the back of the church. And they didn't sound like regular tongues either. I thought, *Son, he's done gone into Indian dialects! This is bad!*

I thought, *That's it! It's over!* I guess five seconds went by like this while those couples stood there looking at me, but it seemed more like five hours. I just looked at them, but I wanted to tell them, *I didn't say that. God said that. That isn't my fault—lay this one on God! Don't lay this on Jesse!*

After what seemed like an eternal silence with those four people looking at me, the first woman finally spoke up and said, "It's true. What you said about us is true." Then the man whom I'd pointed to

confirmed it, saying, "Yeah, we've been wife swapping for three years."

Those people confessed! They confessed their sin in front of the whole church. All four of them had been involved in adultery, and the Lord knew it. I didn't know it, but God knew it and they knew it. They probably had a lot of guilt on their heads, but after they confessed, they knelt down and gave their lives to God. Oh, it was a great time. It caused revival in that church.

Now, let me tell you what I did. I left the service that night, got to my hotel room and said, "God, come here. I want to talk to you, God. Don't ever do that again! Never! I almost had a heart attack when You did that!" Here I was telling God what to do, like I was some kind of big shot! I said, "Why did You make me do that?"

God said, *They repented.*

"Yeah," I said, "but if You want to talk about adultery in front of a church, You tell them Yourself! Leave me out of this situation. Or let me say something like, 'I think there is a person here who has committed adultery.' But don't make me stick my finger in somebody's face and call him an adulterer!"

I mean, I got mad at God. I thought God had pulled a fast one on me, but He wasn't worried about that. He said, *They repented! And you're growing, Jesse.*

"I don't want to grow like this!" I growled.

Let me tell you what God was saying to me. He was telling me that I had been to the Holy of Holies, that I had gone beyond John's baptism and into a deeper revelation of God.

Then He went on to tell me, *Whatever I do is fine. And don't you ever correct Me again!*

"You have to understand us, Lord," I replied. "We're just little, bitty people down here. Do You understand?"

You see, we need to cooperate with God and learn to trust Him. It will sometimes stretch us, but God always knows what we can handle. For quite a few years after that experience, a lot of powerful things would begin to begin to happen, and I would say, "Come on, God. Let's move."

Sometimes He'd say, "No, no, you can't handle that."

But I reminded God that He had told me I'd moved into a deeper revelation and that I wanted more of Him. Sometimes God would move the way I thought He would, and sometimes He didn't. God always knows the best way to get through to His

people. Sometimes ministering to others requires us to take risks, acting by faith in God that what we're saying is really Him.

God told me, *If you're going to walk like I walk and talk like I talk, you've got to live dangerously, son. Christians have always had to live dangerously.*

By the way, the night after I accused those couples of committing adultery, we had a packed church. You couldn't have gotten one more person inside that place. It was packed out, man. People were standing around, because there weren't enough seats to sit in.

The funny thing is, nobody sat on that front row! Stay away from that front row! It's dangerous up there.

very close, swollen veins (varicose)
*"If dem women would walk
in de marsh lak dey used to,
dey wouldn't have dem **very close** vein!"*

45

Catty Women

Women are phenomenal people. They really are. That's not to say that I really ever understood one of them, but they are phenomenal people. But I'll tell you one thing—they sure don't have the same nature as a man.

Take a man noticing another man, for instance. If a man sees another man whose built really well—you know, like Arnold Schwarzenegger—he thinks, *Wow. Look at that guy! He's huge. He must work out all day long. I wish I were big like that. Shoot, if I had muscles like that.... Man, just look at how built that guy is!*

Now women are not like that. A woman will see another woman who's got a good figure—you know, real good, shapely figure. And they don't just think something about it; they *say* it to whomever is with them: "Look at her. Just who does she think she is, walking around strutting like that? I wouldn't wear that. She's just trying to get everybody's attention."

You know what I'm talking about! Any man who's ever walked through the mall with a woman knows what I'm talking about!

But it's important for us to notice other people's good points and not be upset by them. Now, I'm not saying men are better than women or women are better than men, but being irritated over someone else's good qualities isn't good at all. If you look at someone else and get angry because of what you see, check your heart for envy.

It could be that the person has a nice body, a nice car, a nice house, or maybe they're just plain nice. But no matter what they have that you don't, don't let yourself fall into a state of envy. Envy is a sin. That's why one of the Ten Commandments is **Thou shalt not covet.** (Ex. 20:17.) And God put that in the Bible for a reason.

Remember, God will bless you when you put His principles to work, regardless of what area you choose to work on in your life. He will honor your faith and commitment! So, don't be envious of another's good points. It just may be that they've been working on that area for long, long time.

Jesse's Mother Velma's Seafood Gumbo

    1   large onion, chopped
    3   pounds raw shrimp, peeled
    1   pint crab meat
    ⅓   cup cooking oil
    ⅓   cup flour
        filé (Creole seasoning) to taste

In a 5-8 quart pot, make a roux: cover bottom of pot with vegetable oil and add flour. Stir frequently on medium heat until dark brown. Stir in onions and cook until browned. Add 10 ounces of water. Bring to boil for 10 minutes to sauté onions. Fill pot halfway with water and add remaining ingredients. Boil for 20-25 minutes. Turn off heat. Sprinkle filé lightly on top. Stir pot to mix filé, and then cover for 10 minutes. Lift cover and skim excess grease off. Stir. Serve with hot rice.

46

Hatchet-Head

As a father, I never had anything in my heart that made me think, *I'm going to beat this kid's brains out. I'm going to rip her head off.* Now, later I thought that about Jodi's boyfriends, but never her.

Speaking of Jodi's boyfriends, I remember one of the boys who came over one day. That was the ugliest boy I'd ever seen! His head looked like a hatchet. It was shaved on both sides and only had hair growing in a stripe on the top and back. I didn't want my grandbabies to be chopping wood with their heads! I looked at that boy and said, "You've got to go, son!"

I'm telling you, that boy had the ugliest face. And his head was big, too. If he faced you straight on, he looked like a fish, with eyes on the sides of its head. I thought, *Boy, your mamma must've had a hard time delivering you!*

I looked at that boy and said, "You have got to get out!"

I ran him off, man. Then another time a different boy came to the door looking for Jodi, but he didn't look too much better than hatchet-head. Jodi came downstairs and said, "Daddy, was that for me?"

"No," I said, "that was definitely not for you!"

You have to protect your children!

Now, it was probably wrong for me to do that, but then, he didn't marry her either. Glory to God! I didn't want them to fall in love because love is blind. And although love may be blind, sometimes it wakes up twenty years later and says, *Gaaaaa! I can't believe I married this person!*

Let me tell you something else about love. You don't pick who you fall in love with. You don't pick your spouse. How many single people are out there right now trying to pick their own spouses?

If you're single and you see a good-looking girl or guy, you want to get that person's attention. Now, how do you get their attention without looking like an idiot or saying something stupid? You want to be cool and confident, because you want to form a relationship.

So you try and find somebody who will introduce you to this good-looking person, when you really want to just walk up and say, "Hi. I've got to meet you."

When a guy sees a foxy lady, he doesn't want to just rush up and start blabbing. He doesn't want her to think he's a fool, too forward or plain dumb. So there is a little fear there. Think about it.

He just wants to get close to this mamma. He wants to act cool, like, "What's happenin', Mamma?" But he doesn't want to say the wrong thing or sound stupid. So there is a little fear there, but once he makes that step, he decreases the fear.

You might go somewhere and get a Coke, for example, or go hang out with a bunch of people. That's how relationships are formed. You begin to talk to one another, and you start having dates. At this point, let me tell you what the boy is thinking. He's thinking, *Should I kiss her?*

Now, don't lie, guys, because that is a fact, and you know it. You're waiting for the end of the date. You don't care what happens before the end of the date. You're waiting to get to that door. "Come here, Mamma! I'm going to lip-lock you tonight!"

There's no use lying about it, because that is simply the truth. That is human nature. Don't act like you don't know what I'm talking about.

But notice, as you begin to form a relationship with someone, fellowship begins to takes place. This is

when you can really let that girl see you the way you really are. Or, ladies, you let that guy see you the way you really are—without the makeup. He sees you without the sweet-smelling stuff. When you finally see each other then, you think that person is someone else completely. What happened?

You get to that point at which you're honest with the other person. You don't try to hide things. For example, the woman might think, *If he doesn't like me the way I am, bless God, he can go somewhere else. He can take what he gets. This is it, Jack!*

It's called marriage! That beautiful girl you married might someday get up wearing a housecoat that a dog wouldn't sleep on. And her breath could knock a maggot down, boy. I'm not kidding you! That's reality! When you get to this point, you're living in reality.

You start saying things like, "What do you want, honey?"

"I want you to fix me breakfast?"

"Fix it yourself, baby."

That's called reality. But if you're in love, that's called fellowship. See, then it doesn't make any differ-ence what you look like to each other, glory to God. You're being yourself, the way you really are.

You have to see God the way He really is too. You will get to a point in your relationship with God when you're not hiding anything from Him. You know you can be totally honest with Him, because He's seen you at your worst, and He still loves you. He's not going to reject you now. If He were going to reject you, it would've happened before this point in your relationship!

God's Word says in Hebrews 13:5 that He will never leave you nor forsake you—no matter what!

violet, raging, disorderly, violent.

*"When ah told him he pay too much for dat boat, he got **violet**."*

47

HUNTiNG WiTH SiNNERS

I once went hunting in Colorado with twelve of the biggest sinners you've ever seen. Some of you may say, "Why didn't you just go hunting with twelve Christians?"

But I didn't want to go hunting with Christians. I didn't want to go on a Christian hunting trip. I wanted to go hunting with sinners.

I told one of the men who helped gather the hunters together, "I want to go on this hunting trip with the biggest sinners you've got."

"Son," he said, "we've got a crew that goes every year. They're going to talk about women. They're going to drink booze. I mean, it's going to be bad. They'll be telling dirty jokes from the minute you get there."

"That's the crew I want," I said.

"Well, we're sure not going to tell them you're a preacher," he told me.

"No," I said, "go ahead and tell them." I wanted them to know they were going hunting with a preacher.

Sure enough, everyone was told that they were going hunting with a preacher. They all basically said, "Well, I'll tell you one blankety-blank thing. It ain't going to stop our blankety-blank having fun. We don't care if that blankety-blank preacher is coming. We're going to blank whatever we want to blank!"

That's what they really thought. They absolutely weren't going to change their actions because of me.

So the time came for us to go hunting. All of us got together, and when it came time to introduce me, I was introduced as "Reverend Jesse." As soon as I was introduced to those men, they told me, "Now, Reverend, let us just tell you one blankety-blank thing. We're going to blankety-blank talk the way we want to. Do you understand? We're going to talk about women. We're going to talk about drinking, and all of that stuff. We're going to cuss when we want to, and we're going to drink booze. In fact, we have two quarts of Jack Daniel's right here, and we're going up the mountain. If you want to drink some, we won't tell anybody."

I listened to those guys, and when they were done saying what they had to say, I spoke up. I said, "Guys, you all can talk about anything you want and

cuss as much as you want. I couldn't care less." They just looked at me. They were shocked to hear this. They hadn't expected a preacher to say that.

I went on, "If you want to flat cuss, then cuss from the minute you start on the trip to the minute it's over. It doesn't make any difference to me. You can talk about all of your sexual exploits. Most of them are lies anyway, and you know it." They all laughed when I said that.

"Yeah, yeah, yeah," I said, "you're all lying anyway. But you can say whatever you want to say. It doesn't make any difference to me. As a matter of fact, don't let me disturb your lifestyle at all."

"But let me just say this. Since you can cuss when you want and talk about what you want, then if I want to praise God when I want, and if I want to shout praises when I want, then I guess that will be all right."

"That's blankety-blank all right with us," they agreed.

"Well, praise God," I said. "That's what we'll do."

Sure enough, we started hunting that first day, and son, I want to tell you something. They were cussing up a storm. And every time they did, I'd go, "Glory! Whew! Thank You, Jesus!"

They'd go, "Blankety-blank, really! Why did you do that? And why did you blankety-blank shout it so loudly?"

"Whew!" I said. "Because Jesus is in my life!"

God was with me on that hunting trip. I would wake up in the morning and start shouting, "Jesus, thank You, Lord!" I was praising God, and those guys heard it. I'd wake them all up by saying, "Whoa, Lord! Jesse's up! Hello, Jesus!"

By the third day into the hunt, none of those guys had shot anything, but I'd already bagged an elk and a deer. And when those guys saw that, they were surprised. They said, "Blankety-blank! Reverend got the biggest blankety-blank elk we ever saw in this place!"

About that time they were getting a little jealous. They wanted what I had, but they didn't know how to get it. They even asked me, "Hey, Rev, can you talk to the good Lord and help us out here on this hunt?"

"Well," I said, "He'd have been here the entire time, but every time He tries to come, you all just shut Him out by using that foul language all the time. Maybe if you changed your conversation a little bit, He might come down here and say something."

"Do you think so?" they asked.

"Well, I got my elk and deer, didn't I?" I said.

They smiled, and one of them opened up and said, "Help us, God."

You see, I knew I was going to get that elk and deer before the rest of them got anything. I also knew that once I got my kill, I was going to spend the rest of my time witnessing. I knew that by the Holy Ghost. That was why I wanted to go on that hunt.

And that's what I would do. After I shot the elk and deer, I walked all around those woods. I'm not the kind of man who likes to wait in a tree stand for the deer to come to me. I have too much energy to just sit there; I'm going to walk. So I walked up and down those mountains, even past the timberline—the point at which trees don't grow anymore. I went up as high as 11,000 feet chasing elk, and I always made sure I would walk past one of the other guy's stands.

When I walked past any of the others, I would usually hear one of them call me over. For example, when I walked past one guy, he said, "Hey, Rev. Hey, Rev, come here."

"Hey, what's up?" I said.

"Did you see anything?" He was talking about the hunt.

"I haven't seen anything yet," I said.

"Hey, listen. I like you, Reverend. Don't tell the other guys," he said, "but what about this Jesus?"

"Well, I like you too," I said.

"This is really real to you, isn't it?" he asked.

"Yeah," I said. "It's great just to know God."

"Well, you know," he said, "I was raised...."
And he named his denomination.

"Well, that's all right," I told him.

"I don't know if all this stuff is true."

All of them would say things like this sooner or later. I'd go by their stands, because I knew where everybody was hunting. So I'd walk by, and every one of them would call me over and say something like, "Hey, Rev, I want you to pray with me, but don't tell nobody."

I would say, "I'm not going to say a word to anyone else." And I would pray with each one. I was witnessing to them. The light that was in me was brighter than the darkness in them. They tried to spread their darkness around by cussing and telling dirty jokes, but the Light was stronger.

That hunting trip was years ago. Today, eleven of those twelve guys are deacons in a church. One of them is even a preacher! Those men are in church, serving the Lord.

What does that tell you? When you get around sin, don't let sin pull you in. You pull the person out of sin. Jesus called us to be lights *in* the world. There's no way we can keep ourselves away *from* the world. We're not supposed to! Jesus said that we are in the world but not of it. That means that we're not supposed to run from sinners.

Jesus didn't run from sinners. In fact, he had dinner with them. The Bible says that Jesus went over to a man's house and ate dinner with tax collectors and sinners. Why did He do that? Jesus told us why. He said, **"Those who are well have no need of a physician, but those who are sick. I did not come to call the righteous, but sinners, to repentance"** (Mark 2:17 NKJV).

Remember that you are the light of the world because you have Jesus inside you. Light exposes darkness, so let your light shine wherever you go.

Jesse's Mother-in-Law Irene's Shrimp Boulettes

4 cups raw shrimp, peeled
2 medium potatoes
1 egg
1 large onion
½ cup parsley
½ cup green onion tops
1 tablespoon of garlic
   salt and pepper to taste
1 tablespoon of biscuit mix
½ cup cooking oil
½ cup water

Place shrimp, potatoes, onion and garlic in food processor and blend together. Pour mixture in a large mixing bowl and add remaining ingredients. Mix well. Pour oil into a large skillet and heat to medium high. Drop mixture by large spoonfuls (about ¼ cup) into skillet and brown on both sides. Remove and set aside. Drain oil from skillet and place browned patties back in skillet on high heat. Add ½ cup water and bring to a boil. Turn heat on low, cover and simmer for 30 minutes.

48

MaMMa, Me, JiMMY aND MExicO

Let me tell you something. Before I was saved, I couldn't sin without God telling my mamma about it. Mamma had made Jesus her future so much that God would tell her when I was sinning. That aggravated the socks off me. I could be seven hundred miles away from Mamma, and she would know when I was sinning.

I'll give you an example. I was down in Reynosa, Mexico, one time, and Mamma was in New Orleans, Louisiana. I was in my twenties, and I was living like a devil from hell. My drummer and I were in a night-club where women were dancing nude on the tables, and everyone was drinking and smoking dope. I was sinning, and I liked it. I was having a good time down there in Mexico.

In the middle of all this sinning, the phone rang at the bar. Someone answered the phone and called

out, "Is there a Jesse Duplantis here?" I was getting a phone call at a junky old bar in Reynosa, Mexico! Can you believe it? And do you know who it was? It was Mamma. My mamma found me in a bar in Reynosa, Mexico. Now, how would she even know where I was?

I picked up the phone and said, "Hello?" I didn't know who could possibly be calling me.

I heard a familiar voice say, "I see you over there with those sluts! I see you!"

I said, "What? What?" I couldn't believe it was Mamma.

She said, "The Lord showed me where you were, you heathen from hell! God told me to tell you, 'Get out of there!'"

"Okay, Mamma!" I said "See you later! Bye!" I hung the phone up, bless God. I told Jimmy, my drummer, "Get out! Get out! Mamma's going to call fire down! Mamma is going to burn us all!"

He went, "Whoa!" And we took off, man! We left the country and came back across the border into Texas! We got back over to a hotel in McAllen, Texas, and I called Mamma. The first thing I said was, "How did you know?"

"You can't do anything without my knowing about it!" she said. "I told God to tell me every dirty thing you do! I'm praying for you, boy!"

"Mamma," I said, "I never asked you to pray for me."

"It doesn't make any difference," she said. "You're too stupid to ask me to pray for you!"

"Now, Mamma, I don't want to start an argument with you."

"Don't start arguing *with me,* son!" she said. "I'll put my hand through this phone and slap your face!"

Boy, I took the phone away from my face when she said that. Knowing how God told Mamma every-thing I did, I figured He could go, *whap! whap!* right through that phone!

My friend, Jimmy, asked me how Mamma could do that. I told him that God talks to her.

He said, "Whoa, you mean *God?*"

"Yeah, God," I said.

"You mean, God is telling her what we're doing right now?" Jimmy asked.

"Probably."

"Well, let's quit," he told me. He figured it would be easier to just quit sinning than to keep on getting caught by Mamma all the time.

I am not exaggerating. I couldn't do anything bad without Mamma knowing about it. How could she do that? How did Mamma know every time I sinned?

Because Mamma made Jesus her Lord. And He told her everything I was doing. You can't lie to her when God is telling her everything. And I mean everything!

For example, I'd call her and say, "Hey, Mamma. How are you doing?"

She'd say, "I saw you last night."

"Yeah? What was I doing?"

"You were wearing a red–and-white striped shirt," she told me.

"I was?" I asked. "What color pants was I wearing?" In those days you wore colored pants and everything.

"You had those white jeans on," she said.

It was true! I'd had on a red-and-white striped shirt and white jeans just like Mamma described.

"And you were lying to that girl while you were drinking with her," she went on.

"What was her name?" I asked.

"Linda."

"You know her, don't you, Mamma? How do you know her?"

"The Lord told me her name was Linda, and He told me you lied to her," Mamma said. "I asked the Lord to let me see what you were up to, and when I saw that, it hurt my feelings."

"Well," I said, "I didn't mean to hurt your feelings."

"You didn't hurt my feelings because of the girl," she said. "You hurt my feelings because you won't accept Jesus."

"Mamma, I'm just not into this God stuff. You don't understand."

"Jesse," she said, "if He wasn't real, then how would I know all these things?"

"I don't know," I said. "I think you belong to the FBI. You might be a CIA agent. I don't know. You are a covert woman. I don't know how you know these things, but you do."

"Well, I don't want you to go to hell," she told me. "So get saved. Bye."

You see, Mamma was trying to look out for me. She wanted me to stop sinning and running around with the wrong people.

I took a girl over to my mother's house one time, and Mamma took one look at her and said she looked like Jezebel. I didn't take girls home very often, but I thought this one looked pretty good. She was greasy looking, but otherwise she looked all right. But Mamma said to her face, "She looks like a Jezebel!"

Thank God this girl didn't know who Jezebel was.

"Who's Jezebel?" she asked.

"Oh, that's a very nice person we know who lives down the street," I said. "A very pretty lady."

"What's the matter with you, Mamma?" I asked.

"I'll not have those sluts in my house!" she told me right in front of this girl. Mamma didn't like that girl, so I stopped taking her over to the house. But the next girl I brought home, Mamma did like.

The first time I took Cathy over to Mamma's house, Mamma looked at Cathy and said, "That's her." Mamma had never seen Cathy before in her life. I'd actually only taken Cathy by the house because I had to stop in and get something. We were just dropping by when Mamma met Cathy for the first time.

Mamma said, "This is the woman you're going to marry."

"Mamma," I said, "come here. I don't want to marry this girl. I just want to date her."

"The Lord has already told me, Jesse. She's the girl. That's her. It's over with. I know who your wife is going to be."

After that, Mamma started to go to work on Cathy to get her saved. She started working on Cathy, and Cathy did get saved. Cathy called Mamma up one day and told her so. Mamma said, "Well, put that heathen on the phone."

I got on the phone and said, "Yeah, Mom, what do you want?"

"We're going to get you next," she said. "Yeah, we're going to get you."

"I understand that, Mamma," I said.

What made Mamma do that? She made Jesus a real part of her life. I'm telling you, Mamma made Jesus so much a part of her life that she was always saying something about God. Jesus was her future, and Jesus was going to be the future of her children and grandchildren, the future of her family. Through her prayers she brought all of us to the knowledge of God—every one of us. We were a bunch of heathens before we got saved. We were some devils.

But, because Mamma kept on praying for her family like that, we all got saved. One person who persevered in prayer over her loved ones made that much of a difference.

Do you have people you love who are not saved? This story can help you, because it shows you the power of one person's prayers. Don't ever give up on praying and witnessing to lost loved ones in your family. God will honor your prayers.

warse, stinging insect
"He's mean lak a warse."

49

THE SPEEDING SHERIFF

Several years ago, the Lord used a speeding sheriff to teach me the importance of perception. The airline I flew on arrived late. Really late. I was scheduled to preach, and as I looked at my watch, I could visualize the people crowding into the church. I knew the pastor would be pacing in his office, wondering when my flight would get in. The people would be singing for at least an hour before I could get there. I imagine that the pastor would begin feeling pretty desperate, not wanting his congregation to suffer from the common worship service dilemma—too much clapping.

And I believe that is why he sent the fastest-driving member of his congregation to the airport to pick me up—the one person who could sail through traffic at record-breaking speed without fear of death or a ticket. That's right, he sent the sheriff. And man, when I tell you that this guy could drive, I mean, this guy could *drive!*

The first words out of his mouth were, "Reverend Duplantis, are you afraid of speed?"

"No, sir," I said.

"Well, my pastor told me to get you to the church in a hurry, and the only man who can do that is me. Pastor said they're going to sing until you get there. So hold on!"

He turned the red and blue lights on, and we began to move! The siren was screaming, and he was competing with it. Both of them were belting out a shrill "Get out of the way!" the whole ride there.

I dug my nails, what little I had, into the vinyl and watched the speedometer climb. Seventy-five. Ninety-two. One hundred and one. One hundred and ten. One hundred and twenty. When he hit one hundred and thirty, I just about ripped out a handful of vinyl and foam. I kept switching my hands back and forth from the seat to the seat beats. I was grabbing just about anything that looked like it would hold and praying in tongues under my breath! He looked over at me and said, "Should I bow my head?"

I said, "No, no! You keep your eyes open—don't worry about me!"

I ain't going to lie! I had huge goosebumps of fear scratching at my pant legs!

He was flying up on cars left and right. It seemed like he'd get so close to their bumpers that we were going to crash right into them. Then he'd just swerve over into the other lane and pass them, almost knocking the side-view mirror off when he did.

I said, "Sir, sir—!" I kept thinking, *This guy is going to plow into the back of these cars! Please, Lord, don't let the sheriff kill me on the way to the meeting!*

The sheriff must have read my mind, because right after I thought that he tried to comfort me.

"Don't worry," he said. "I'm not going to hit this car."

"Suppose they tap their brakes?" I asked boldly.

He grinned and shook his head. "I'm looking at the person ahead of me. A good policeman will never look at the car he's chasing; he'll look ahead of it. He is already envisioning what the car ahead of that one is going to do."

I relaxed just a little. And I began to think about what he'd said. I'd just watched him pass three cars at record speed. The whole time my eyes were on bumpers and side mirrors. His eyes, as he said, were on the road ahead of us. He was looking farther out. Sure he could see the cars directly in front of us, but his attention lay beyond them. While I was staring at

the present dangers, he was already envisioning what lay ahead.

The Lord spoke to me as I thought of what the sheriff had said. And thank God He did, because I sure needed some help! Through that sheriff's words, God showed me that one of the problems with believers is that we always seem to stare at the back of the "car" we're chasing. Fixed on what is going on in the present, we seldom give thought to the soon-coming future.

Now that doesn't mean we need to be in la-la land, pretending never to see what is going on around us at the time. No way! That should never happen! Just like that policeman, we should be aware of what is around us at all times. But our eyes shouldn't be so focused on what is going on right this second that we forget to look ahead to the destiny God has planned for our lives.

As a believer, you should look at the present. You should recognize it and deal with it as it comes along. But it alone shouldn't monopolize your attention. If you want to be successful in this life, if you want to be known for having an excellent spirit and you want to experience all the blessing it brings, practice giving attention to what is further down the road.

Your life is a journey. And on the road from your birth to death, God has planned a destiny for you that is as rewarding as it is fulfilling. If you will develop a spirit of excellence, the Lord will guide you towards that destiny. With excellence of spirit working in your life, you enable Him to help you live your destiny in peace and joy.

Only Jesus can help us to see what is ahead with *clarity.* Only Jesus can give us the *perception* we need in order to move towards our destiny without getting off course and losing our peace. How do we gain that perception? Through developing an excellent spirit. And how do we develop an excellent spirit? By living a life of purpose and prayer.

So you may ask, "What exactly is perception?" Well, in practical terms, it's the ability to know what is really going on in the spirit realm. People who have perception are submitted to God, and it's evident in everything they do and say. Because they are submitted to God and His Word, they can be trusted with certain spiritual attributes.

When you have spiritual perception, you will be very sensitive to God's prompting. You'll have a keen insight into the spirit realm and have clear vision when confronted with a crisis in life.

Think of it like that sheriff who was trained to
see beyond the car in front of him and to anticipate
the situations that would soon arise. Spiritual perception can be like that. The Holy Spirit may impress you
to say something that someone else needs to hear. He
may give you a vision or a dream of things to come.
He may simply give you insight to a critical situation.
In any case, He shows us how to look out ahead of us
and anticipate the destiny God has planned for each of
our lives.

Jesse's Mother-in-Law Irene's Shrimp Jambalaya

3 tablespoons vegetable oil
3 cups raw shrimp, peeled
3 large onions, chopped
¼ cup of salt meat, finely chopped
3 cups of raw rice
6 cups water
   salt and pepper to taste

   In a large non-stick pot add oil and onions.
Cook on medium high heat until onions turn dark
brown, stirring constantly. Add salt meat and cook
for 5 minutes longer. Add 3 tablespoons of water and
sauté for 5 minutes or until the meat starts to fry. Stir
in the shrimp and cook until the shrimp start to fry.
Add rice and cook for 5 minutes before adding water.
Cook uncovered until it comes to a full boil. Stir well,
cover and cook on low for 20 minutes. Do not uncover
during this cooking time. Lift lid and gently blend
with a large cooking fork, being careful not to pack
the rice and shrimp mixture. Replace lid and cook an
additional 10 minutes or until rice is tender.

50

Making intercession

God speaks to your spirit through an inner witness. Do you know what I mean by an inner witness? Well, let me give you a prime example of something that happened to me years ago.

I got up one morning, and everything was going well in my life. My personal life was fine. My business life, social life and public life were all fine. The ministry was great, and everything else was wonderful. To tell you the truth, I thought it was going to be a great day.

But soon after I got up a heaviness came on me, that blah kind of feeling you sometimes get. I don't know how else to say it. I wasn't sick in my body, and I wasn't depressed. I just felt this heaviness on the inside of me. So I began to rebuke the devil.

"Get out of here, devil," I commanded. "I come against you in Jesus' name. I *bind* you. I *bind* you, devil from hell. Get out of here!" But, instead of going

away, the feeling got worse and worse. I just got
heavier, even though there was nothing wrong with me.

I must have bound the devil for about thirty-five
minutes, and nothing happened. Finally, the Lord said,
Jesse! I knew that voice.

"What?" I said.

What are you doing? He asked me.

"I'm over here binding the devil, Lord," I said.

No, you're not. You're binding Me, He told me.

"I'm binding You?" I asked.

*Yes, that feeling in your spirit is Me. I want to use
your spirit right now to make utterances and groanings that
cannot be mentioned. That's the Spirit of God inside of you,
not the devil.*

What happened was that the Holy Spirit wanted
to making intercession through my spirit with utter-
ings and groanings that could not be mentioned—and
I was binding it. I was binding God, thinking it was
the devil. How many of you have ever experienced
such a thing? It's in the Bible: **Likewise the Spirit
also helps in our weaknesses. For we do not know
what we should pray for as we ought, but the Spirit
Himself makes intercession for us with groanings
which cannot be uttered** (Rom. 8:26 NKJV).

Don't always assume that the weight you sometimes feel inside is the devil. Oftentimes the Holy Ghost will move upon you like He did me. He may give you deep, deep urging to pray for someone who may be in trouble. It might be somebody in China or a brother in Siberia who is going through a wasteland. It could be for *yourself* that you're praying. The important thing is that you realize you're hearing from God, and those groanings on the inside are from Him, not the devil.

If the Holy Ghost moves on you to pray like that, be sure to pray long enough for the heaviness to lift off you. You will get to the point where you're released from that burden to pray, and when that happens, it means you've done your work. Whatever it was you were praying for has been resolved, and God will get all the glory.

weakling, to move from side to side

*"Stop **weakling** T-Boy, de
Preese is looking at you."*

51

YELLOW WATER TEMPTATION

Years ago, I was in Dallas, and my wife and I stopped at a restaurant to grab a bite to eat. When the waitress came to the table to get our drink orders, I asked for water, and soon after the waitress brought me a glass.

Although the water was a little yellow, I didn't pay any mind. When you travel as much as I do, you know that water is different everywhere you go. Some places have yellow water, while others have light brown. The worst water in the world is in Monroe, Louisiana. Their water is so oily, it slips down your throat before you can taste it! They may call it artesian, but I call it polluted.

Anyway, I didn't really pay any attention to what shade of yuck the water was the waitress had just brought to the table. I just thought, *Well, maybe*

that is the way their water is. So I took that glass and swigged back a mouthful. And when I did, I tasted scotch and water. I was shocked. I held that booze in my mouth, not knowing what to do. I hadn't tasted scotch in years. Then I yielded to the flesh a little. I leaned my head back and gargled. Cathy's eyes darted to my throat.

Her eyebrow shot to the sky as she slowly hissed, "Spit it out. Spit it out *now!*"

I held it in my mouth.

"Spit it out!" she said again—but this time with a little more intensity in her voice. I started looking around for somewhere to spit. The devil said, *Swallow it.*

I thought, *Naaa, I'm not going to swallow it. But I'll just hold it in my mouth for a while.* I hadn't felt that burn on my throat in years.

I heard my wife again, but this time she was growling, "Spit it out! I don't care if you spit it on the floor! You spit it out!" She was staring me down bad!

So I grabbed my glass from the table and spit right back into it. "This is...this is...*terrible*," I said, not so convincingly.

"Don't you lick your fingers!" my wife scowled. "Give me those fingers, bless God!"

I called the waitress over. "That's liquor," I said, pointing.

"Well, didn't you ask for scotch and water?"

"No, I asked for water. I'm a preacher!"

"Oh," she said, but she didn't look that startled that she'd just served scotch to a preacher. I wondered how many had been there drinking.

"Ma'am," I said, "I used to drink a lot years ago, but I don't do that now."

She didn't say anything, but she went and got me a new glass, except this time it was filled with water, clear as crystal.

That day was a big temptation for me. I believe that had I not had a fierce loyalty to God, I would not have had the anchorage I needed to spit that scotch out. You see, as I mentioned before, I'd been a big drinker before I gave my life to God. And no matter how much my wife would've griped, if I hadn't considered what God had done for me, I probably would have swallowed that booze like it was no big deal. I probably would have thought, *So what? One swallow of scotch won't kill me!*

But do you know what? That kind of reasoning wasn't available to me, because a long time ago I made a decision to be a man of principle. It was principle that kept me from breaking the promise I made to the Lord back in 1974—the promise that I'd never drink or do drugs again if He'd only come into my life and change me.

But do you know what? I never had to work at keeping that promise. Jesus supernaturally delivered me from my addictions to alcohol and drugs. He rehabilitated me in about ten seconds flat when I gave my life to Him. No withdrawals, no shakes, no sweats—nothing but freedom!

Now, how could I hurt my Jesus by going back on my promise? I couldn't! My loyalty to Jesus is just too strong to let some hell-bent flesh ruin what He has done for me! It is loyalty that makes me say no to temptation.

How about you? Do you feel that your loyalty to Jesus is so strong that it anchors you down when the winds of temptation blow? Do you feel in your heart that you are a person of principle, willing to resist temptation in order to please God?

If you are the least bit unsure, take time to pray and ask God to help you out. Ask Him to renew your spirit by His Word and to help you be a faithful person who is uncompromisingly loyal to His Word. He'll do it! God loves you! He cares about your life, no

matter what is going on. I know God can change you, just like He changed me those many years ago.

No, God's not finished with me yet. I'm still growing and learning, even though I'm a preacher. God's still working on me. Day by day, I just live my life and read my Bible and talk to Jesus. He's my friend, a part of my everyday life.

That's what I hope Jesus will become for you—a friend who is part of your everyday life. That's the beauty of a personal relationship with God. It can get you through all of life's crazy challenges and turn you into something better than you ever thought you could be. It can help you be a person of principle who has fun living life too!

JESSE'S MOTHER VELMA'S SMOTHERED POTATOES

3 pounds potatoes, diced
1 medium onion, diced
   vegetable oil (see directions for amount)

Cover bottom of 10-inch iron pot with vegetable oil.

Brown onions. Add potatoes. Season to taste. Cover pot and fry on low heat until potatoes are tender and brown.

Stir occasionally, being careful not to break up the potatoes.

Jesse Duplantis is what some would call a true evangelist. Supernaturally saved and delivered from a life of addiction in 1974 and called by God to the office of the evangelist in 1978, he founded Jesse Duplantis Ministries with one mission in his mind and one vision in his heart—global evangelism, whatever the cost. And throughout his many years of evangelistic ministry, he has sought to do just that.

With a television ministry that spans the globe, ministry offices in America, the United Kingdom and Australia and a preaching itinerary that has taken him to over 1000 different churches to date, Jesse is still fulfilling his original call to evangelism with gusto! His commitment to Christ, long-standing integrity in ministry and infectious, joyful nature have made him one of the most loved and respected ministers of the gospel today. Oral Roberts Ministries recognized his achievements in the field of evangelism by awarding him an honorary doctorate of divinity in 1999.

A Cajun from Southern Louisiana, Jesse makes the Bible easy to understand by preaching its truths in our everyday vernacular and spicing his messages with humor. Often called the "Apostle of Joy" because of hilarious illustrations, Jesse's anointed preaching and down-to-earth style have helped to open the door for countless numbers of people to receive Jesus as their Lord and Savior. Jesse has proven through his own life that no matter who you are or where you come from, God can change your heart, develop your character through His Word and help you find and complete your divine destiny.

To contact Jesse Duplantis Ministries
write or call:

Jesse Duplantis Ministries
P.O. Box 20149
New Orleans, Louisiana 70141
(985) 764-2000
www.jdm.org

*Please include your prayer requests
and comments when you write.*

OTHER BOOKS BY DR. JESSE DUPLANTIS

Wanting A God You Can Talk To
Heaven — Close Encounters of the God Kind
God Is Not Enough, He's Too Much!
The Ministry of Cheerfulness
Running Toward Your Giant
Don't Be Affected by the World's Message
Keep Your Foot on the Devil's Neck
Leave it in the Hands of a Specialist
One More Night With the Frogs
The Battle of Life
What In Hell Do You Want?
The Sovereignty of God

Jesse Duplantis Ministries
New Orleans, LA 70141

Prayer of Salvation

A born-again, committed relationship with God is the key to the victorious life. Jesus, the Son of God laid down His life and rose again so that we could spend eternity with Him in heaven and experience His absolute best on earth. The Bible says, **"For God so loved the world, that he gave his only begotten Son, that whosoever believeth in him should not perish, but have everlasting life"** (John 3:16).

It is the will of God that everyone receive eternal salvation. The way to receive this salvation is to call upon the name of Jesus and confess Him as your Lord. The Bible says, **"That if thou shalt confess with thy mouth the Lord Jesus, and shalt believe in thine heart that God hath raised him from the dead, thou shalt be saved. For whosoever shall call upon the name of the Lord shall be saved"** (Romans 10:9-10,13).

Jesus has given salvation, healing and countless benefits to all who call upon His name. These benefits can be yours if you receive Him into your heart by praying this prayer.

Heavenly Father, I come to You admitting that I am a sinner. Right now, I choose to turn away from sin, and I ask You to cleanse me of all unrighteousness. I believe that Your Son, Jesus died on the cross to take away my sins. I also believe that He rose again from the dead so that I might be justified and made righteous through faith in Him. I call upon the name of Jesus Christ to be the Savior and Lord of my life. Jesus, I choose to follow You, and ask that You fill me with the power of the Holy Spirit. I declare that right now, I am a born-again child of God. I am free from sin, and full of the righteousness of God. I am saved in Jesus' name, Amen.

If you have prayed this prayer to receive Jesus Christ as your Savior, or if this book has changed your life, we would like to hear from you. Please write us at:

Jesse Duplantis Ministries

P.O. Box 20149
New Orleans, LA 70141

You can also visit us on the web at
www.jdm.org